Cambridge Student G

Shakespeare

Hamlet

Rex Gibson

Series Editor: Rex Gibson

CAMBRIDGE
UNIVERSITY PRESS

PUBLISHED BY THE PRESS SYNDICATE OF THE UNIVERSITY OF CAMBRIDGE
The Pitt Building, Trumpington Street, Cambridge, United Kingdom

CAMBRIDGE UNIVERSITY PRESS
The Edinburgh Building, Cambridge CB2 2RU, UK
40 West 20th Street, New York, NY 10011–4211, USA
477 Williamstown Road, Port Melbourne, VIC 3207, Australia
Ruiz de Alarcón 13, 28014 Madrid, Spain
Dock House, The Waterfront, Cape Town 8001, South Africa

http://www.cambridge.org

© Cambridge University Press 2002

This book is in copyright. Subject to statutory exception and to the provisions
of relevant collective licensing agreements, no reproduction of any part may
take place without the written permission of Cambridge University Press.

First published 2002

Printed in the United Kingdom at the University Press, Cambridge

Typeface 9.5/12pt Scala   *System* QuarkXPress®

A catalogue record for this book is available from the British Library

ISBN 0 521 00815 8 paperback

Cover image: © Getty Images/PhotoDisc

SHAKESPEARE CENTRE
83393927
STRATFORD-UPON-AVON

Contents

Introduction   4

Commentary   5

Contexts   55
     What did Shakespeare write?   55
     What did Shakespeare read?   57
     What was Shakespeare's England like?   61
       Politics and the court   64
       Revenge   68
       Incest   69
       Religion   69
       The subordination of women   72
       Theatre   72

Language   74
     Imagery   75
     Doubling   78
     Repetition   79
     Lists   80
     Verse and prose   81
     Soliloquy   83
     Antithesis   83

Critical approaches   85
     Traditional criticism   85
     Modern criticism   91
       Political criticism   92
       Feminist criticism   96
       Performance criticism: the 'afterlife' of *Hamlet*   99
       Psychoanalytic criticism   103
       Postmodern criticism   104

Organising your responses   106
     Writing about an extract   107
     Writing an essay   119
     Writing about character   123
     A note on examiners   125

Resources   126
     Books   126
     Films   128
     Audio books   128
     Hamlet on the Web   128

Introduction

If you call up Shakespeare's *Hamlet* on the World Wide Web you will find over 100,000 items. If you were able to count all the books and articles published about the play you would have a much larger total. Ever since it was first performed around 1601, *Hamlet* has proved immensely popular with audiences. Today it is staged in countries all around the world. Its language and images have become famous and familiar: 'To be or not to be', 'Alas, poor Yorick', Hamlet contemplating the skull.

Why has the play held such fascinating appeal for over 400 years? In spite of all the billions of words written about it, and all its performances, Shakespeare's *Hamlet* remains as enigmatic as Leonardo da Vinci's *Mona Lisa*. Just as people for centuries have tried without success to solve the riddle of the Mona Lisa's smile, so Hamlet has also been endlessly interpreted. But the play has resisted all attempts to pluck out the heart of its mystery.

The seemingly simple question 'What is the play about?' yields a host of answers. One might be that *Hamlet* portrays the inner turmoil of an alienated and melancholy young man, ordered by a ghost to revenge his father's murder. His emotional journey results in great harm to others as he travels from the deeply troubled questioning of 'To be or not to be' to the calm acceptance of 'Let be'. He achieves his revenge almost by accident. Other valid answers include interpreting the play as a family drama, a political thriller about a corrupt society, a revenge tragedy, a study in grief, a profoundly religious tract.

Hamlet's openness to all kinds of possible interpretations make it the most theatrical of plays. It is itself vitally concerned with theatre, full of the language of acting, and of characters who dissemble, pretending to be what they are not.

That theatricality contributes significantly to *Hamlet*'s inexhaustible capacity for being interpreted afresh. This guide will make you familiar with many different ways in which *Hamlet* has been interpreted on the stage and on the page. It will enable you to form your own response and help you see that although the play is deeply rooted in the preoccupations of Elizabethan England, it is still sharply relevant today.

Commentary

Act 1 Scene 1

'Who's there?' For 400 years actors and critics have responded in a dazzling variety of ways to Barnardo's challenge to Francisco that begins the play. Actors face the problem of how to stage the tense atmosphere of this nervous encounter, just after midnight, on the gun platform of Elsinore Castle. In Shakespeare's day, the scene was performed on the Globe stage, without scenery, in the broad daylight of a London afternoon. In nineteenth-century stagings, the two apprehensive sentries met on elaborately constructed Gothic-style battlements. In the twentieth century, Laurence Olivier's film opened in swirling mist, and set the guards' staccato exchanges on a shadowy staircase within the castle's huge stone walls.

For critics, the opening lines have symbolic as well as dramatic significance. The language not only creates the impression of a bitterly cold night, but also ominously foreshadows major themes of *Hamlet*. 'Who's there?' is the first of the many anxious questions that establish the tone of uncertainty that runs through the play. Barnardo's question symbolises the search for personal identity, and for the reality that lies behind outward appearance. Critics also note that the words are spoken by the wrong sentry: it is Francisco, already on guard, who should make the challenge. Barnardo's blunder signifies the mistakes and confusions that will recur as the play unfolds.

Similarly, Barnardo's 'Long live the king!' has been interpreted as a password that makes an ironic comment: the play will present the ghost of a dead king and will report or show the deaths of three other kings (Old Hamlet, Old Fortinbras, Claudius). Even Francisco, who after line 18 vanishes for ever from *Hamlet*, is given critical significance. His enigmatic 'And I am sick at heart' will find an echo in all that follows as the play traces the nature and consequences of Hamlet's own troubled melancholy.

The entry of Horatio intensifies the already taut atmosphere. The guards have invited him to join them, to observe and to question what they have seen twice before on their sentry duty. What have they seen? Marcellus' language deepens the sense of mystery: 'this thing', 'this dreaded sight', 'this apparition'. But Horatio, a scholar and philosopher, is sceptical of the guards' 'fantasy'. He dismisses the possibility of seeing it himself: 'Tush, tush, 'twill not appear.'

The sudden appearance of the Ghost, breaking into Barnardo's foreboding 'The bell then beating one –', abruptly dispels Horatio's scepticism: 'It harrows me with fear and wonder.' Dressed all in armour, the Ghost resembles 'the majesty of buried Denmark': the dead King Hamlet. Horatio demands it speak, but the Ghost stalks away leaving Horatio pale and trembling. He suspects that the dead king's appearance foretells future disasters for Denmark: 'This bodes some strange eruption to our state.'

Horatio's suspicion that the Ghost is an omen of troubles ahead for the state of Denmark seems to imply that the play will be mainly concerned with politics. That impression is deepened as Marcellus asks why sentries are posted each night, and what causes Denmark's urgent preparations for war. Cannons are rolling off the assembly line daily, weapons are purchased from foreign countries, and ships are being built by 'impress of shipwrights': forced labour.

Horatio's explanation sounds like the introduction to a history play. King Hamlet was challenged to personal combat by Fortinbras, king of Norway. Both men wagered large possessions of land on the outcome of the duel. Hamlet slew Fortinbras and took over his lands. Now the king of Norway's son, Young Fortinbras, has 'Sharked up a list of landless resolutes': recruited an army of mercenaries to seize back the lost lands. Horatio feels this explains the frantic activity as the Danes prepare to resist the threatened invasion:

> And this, I take it,
> Is the main motive of our preparations,
> The source of this our watch, and the chief head
> Of this post-haste and romage in the land.   *(lines 104–7)*

Horatio likens the apparition to the ominous signs that preceded the assassination of Julius Caesar: the living dead, comets, bloody rain, sunspots, the eclipse of the moon. In listing such supernatural happenings as forewarners of doom, the scholarly Horatio now seems more superstitious than sceptical. The atmosphere of fearful expectation that his lines generate gives dramatic impetus to the second appearance of the Ghost.

Five times Horatio challenges the Ghost to speak, but at the crowing of the cock, it vanishes. The final speeches of Scene 1 are atmospherically poetic as Horatio explains how cockcrow was the summons for any wandering ghost to return to its prison, and Marcellus claims the cockerel crows all night long at Christmas, a time when no ghost dare walk, nor any harm be done. After a lyrical image of daylight spreading across the horizon like a traveller dressed in a red cloak, Horatio proposes they tell what they have seen to 'young Hamlet'. It is the first mention of the character who from now on will dominate the play:

> But look, the morn in russet mantle clad
> Walks o'er the dew of yon high eastward hill.
> Break we our watch up, and by my advice
> Let us impart what we have seen tonight
> Unto young Hamlet ...   *(lines 166–70)*

Act 1 Scene 2

In the theatre, directors of the play seize the opportunity to stage a striking contrast between Scene 1 and Scene 2. The darkness and the apprehensive atmosphere of the gun platform suddenly transforms to the brilliant spectacle and celebratory mood of Denmark's royal court. The visual contrast between darkness and light reflects the language differences between the openings of the two scenes. Scene 1 began with questions and short, staccato exchanges. Those hesitations and uncertainties contrast with the smooth flow of Claudius' confident opening speech:

> Though yet of Hamlet our dear brother's death
> The memory be green ...   *(lines 1–2)*

The threats of war and political instability evident in Scene 1 now come under Claudius' astute and businesslike command. He deals with three matters: the new regime (the tribute to the dead King Hamlet, and Claudius' own marriage to Gertrude); foreign affairs (Fortinbras' demands); and individual petitions (Laertes and Hamlet both wish to leave Denmark).

Claudius' language, with its elaborate and carefully constructed long sentences, seems assertive and self-assured. But what does such language reveal about him? Some critics find an eloquent dignity in his speeches, appropriate to the ceremony of the state occasion. Other critics suspect Claudius' fluency, and judge him to be shifty and hypocritical in a speech which is too plausible and too balanced to be true. They invite you to consider equivocal features in Claudius' language which suggest inner anxieties: the over-frequent use of the royal 'we', 'us', and 'our'; the too-careful structuring of the speech, suggesting it is an insincere and rehearsed performance; his flattery of the court ('your better wisdoms'); and the antitheses (contrasts) in which he tells of his marriage to Gertrude:

> Have we, as 'twere with a defeated joy,
> With one auspicious and one dropping eye,
> With mirth in funeral and with dirge in marriage,
> In equal scale weighing delight and dole,
> Taken to wife;   *(lines 10–14)*

Critics who see Claudius' insincerity expressed in his language claim to detect a disturbing falseness beneath the formal balance of the lines. They point out that for an Elizabethan audience, the second antithesis ('With one auspicious and one dropping eye') implied deviousness, because a contemporary proverb held that a false man looked up with one eye and down with the other. The other antitheses imply a similar two-facedness: someone who can simultaneously express joy and sorrow, or show an inappropriate emotion at a funeral or a marriage.

Claudius dismisses Fortinbras' demands, 'So much for him', despatches ambassadors to the king of Norway to stop Fortinbras' military venture, and pleasantly grants Laertes leave to return to France. He then turns to Hamlet. Some actors insert a lengthy pause after his first word, 'But', to signify the special problem Claudius feels that his nephew, now his stepson, presents:

> But now my cousin Hamlet, and my son –   *(line 64)*

Hamlet has been on stage from the start of the scene. He is dressed in black, signifying grief for his dead father. His appearance contrasts strikingly with the costumes and attitudes of the courtiers celebrating the wedding of Claudius and Gertrude. Before he speaks, the degree to which his alienation and melancholy is signalled in his behaviour varies from production to production. But when he speaks, he immediately becomes the focus of attention for actors and audience alike, where he remains until the end of the play:

A little more than kin, and less than kind.   *(line 65)*

Hamlet's comment establishes what he thinks of Claudius. They are too closely related ('kin') for Hamlet's liking, but they do not share the same nature ('kind'). His next remark, the only time he speaks directly to Claudius in the scene, again denies any close relationship:

Not so my lord, I am too much i'th'sun.   *(line 67)*

Claudius' marriage to Gertrude has transformed Hamlet from 'cousin' (an Elizabethan term for 'nephew') to 'son', a kinship closer than Hamlet desires. His pun on 'sun' has many possible interpretations: being Claudius' son is too much for him; he prefers the shade of grief to the sunshine of public view; he rejects Claudius as a father; he rejects the warmth of Claudius' favour.

Gertrude implores Hamlet to cease mourning his dead father, but he seizes on her words 'common' and 'seems', turning both into rebukes. In performance, Hamlet often loads the words with bitter irony as he claims to despise pretence: 'I know not seems.' Dressing in black, sighing, weeping, looking sad are the outward actions of mourning that any man might play, but his inner feeling of grief is genuine, for him there is no pretence.

Claudius declares Hamlet his successor as king, but within four lines delivers a judgement which will have enormous consequences for the tragedy: he refuses permission for Hamlet to return to university:

For your intent
In going back to school in Wittenberg,
It is most retrograde to our desire   *(lines 112–14)*

The departure of the court leaves Hamlet alone on stage, presenting a visual image of his isolation. As he struggles with his thoughts and feelings, his language is typical of the self-analysis that will recur in later soliloquies. He:

- longs for death ('O that this too too solid flesh would melt') but knows that suicide is forbidden by the law ('canon') of God ('the Everlasting');
- finds life and the world utterly tedious and foul, overrun with 'things rank and gross';
- recalls his dead father as infinitely superior to Claudius ('Hyperion to a satyr': the sun god to a lecherous creature, half-man, half-goat);
- recalls how tenderly and protectively his father loved his mother, and how passionately she loved him;
- is disgusted with his mother's second marriage to his despised uncle so soon after his father's death;
- condemns the marriage, but sorrowfully vows silence.

By dramatic convention, a character speaks the truth in soliloquy, revealing his or her innermost thoughts and emotions. Hamlet's soliloquy exposes the range of his depression: weariness, despair, grief, anger, nausea, loathing and disgust, resignation. But significantly he is not concerned with the state of Denmark, his prospects of becoming king, or being forbidden to return to Wittenberg. Hamlet's troubled mind is obsessed with family matters: his father, his uncle, and above all, his mother. He is obsessed with the haste of Gertrude's remarriage, and he works himself up to a sibilant expression of sexual disgust:

> Oh most wicked speed, to post
> With such dexterity to incestuous sheets.   *(lines 156–7)*

Hamlet's courteous welcome of Horatio, Marcellus and Barnardo seems to change his mood, but his bitter joke that the leftovers from his father's funeral feast were used for Gertrude's wedding breakfast shows the thought of his mother's hasty marriage still festers in his mind. Amazed by the report of the appearance of his father's ghost, Hamlet closely questions the three men and abruptly decides to watch that night on the gun platform, and to speak to the apparition. His final four-line soliloquy, full of short sentences, mixes surprise, apprehension, suspicion, impatience, and the certainty that evil acts, now hidden, will inevitably be revealed:

My father's spirit, in arms! All is not well.
I doubt some foul play. Would the night were come.
Till then sit still my soul. Foul deeds will rise
Though all the earth o'erwhelm them to men's eyes.

(lines 254–7)

Act 1 Scene 3

Scene 3 establishes more dramatic contrasts. After the tension of the gun platform and the ceremony of the court, the scene shifts to a private home. Hamlet's uneasy relationships with his mother and stepfather uncle have already been exposed. Now the relationships of Polonius' family are laid open to audience scrutiny.

Laertes, about to depart for France, warns Ophelia against thinking that Hamlet has any real affection for her. In formal, elaborate verse, Laertes claims that Hamlet's love will be short-lived, because as he grows older he will become wiser ('the mind and soul / Grows wide withal'). Hamlet cannot choose to marry whoever he wishes ('his will is not his own') because he is a prince, and so must marry in the interest of the state. Public duty comes before private feelings.

The second half of Laertes' speech uses images of treasure, war, masks and disease as sexual metaphors to warn his sister against losing her virginity to Hamlet's 'unmastered importunity'. She reminds him to practise what he preaches, and then Laertes is lectured by his father. Polonius' 'precepts' (moral principles) have been variously interpreted as wise common sense (e.g. choose good friends, be true to yourself) and as self-centred craftiness (e.g. be suspicious of friends and dominate them, think always of your own interests).

Delivering the 'precepts', Polonius has been played in very different ways: serious, comic, pompously aloof, lovingly sincere. A similarly wide range of options is open to Laertes and Ophelia in how they react to their father's advice. Do they listen respectfully, evidently convinced of the wisdom of the precepts? Or do they signal to the audience that they have heard it all before? In some productions brother and sister mouth Polonius' words in silent imitation, or pull faces behind his back, or exchange bored or mocking looks.

The third episode in the scene makes it difficult to portray Polonius sympathetically. He shares Laertes' suspicion and distrust of Hamlet, and exhibits similar anxiety and prurience about sex. He seems overbearing as he remonstrates with Ophelia about her relationship with Hamlet: 'Affection? Puh! You speak like a green girl', and he launches into a moralising sermon, telling his daughter what to think of Hamlet's tenders of affection. He contemptuously disbelieves Hamlet's honesty of intention, dismissing it as merely lustful desire, and he forbids Ophelia to see Hamlet again.

In this scene both men give orders to Ophelia and seek to control her emotions, thoughts and actions. She may choose to respond submissively, or with barely controlled resentment, or in some other way. Her response will have important consequences for the audience's perception of character and family relationships.

Act 1 Scene 4

On the bitingly cold gun platform, Hamlet, Horatio and Marcellus await the Ghost. The noise of trumpets and cannon signalling Claudius' celebrations prompts Hamlet to a condemnation of the drunkenness of the Danes. He reflects that a particular character flaw, 'some vicious mole of nature', can overwhelm reason and dignity. His reflection is an expression of Aristotle's claim that the cause of tragedy is a character flaw in the tragic hero. This 'single cause' explanation neglects many other factors that contribute to tragedy, but the popularity of Aristotle's over-simple theory is evident in Olivier's film of Hamlet which begins with a voice-over: 'This is the tragedy of a man who could not make up his mind'.

Hamlet's meditation on human nature is interrupted by the appearance of the Ghost. He sees it as 'a questionable shape', and the question it poses for him will haunt him for much of the play: is it good or evil? Hamlet's uncertainty whether the Ghost is an agent of God or the Devil is expressed in three vivid antitheses and three final questions:

> Be thou a spirit of health, or goblin damned,
> Bring with thee airs from heaven or blasts from hell,
> Be thy intents wicked or charitable   *(lines 40–2)*

> Say, why is this? wherefore? What should we do?   *(line 57)*

The Ghost beckons Hamlet to follow, and he does so, resisting Horatio's and Marcellus' attempts to restrain him: 'My fate cries out'.

In performance, Hamlet often holds his sword hilt like a cross before his face as if to defend himself from evil. That gesture, the ambiguous nature of the Ghost, and Marcellus' line help create the sense of corruption that will grow increasingly through the play:

> Something is rotten in the state of Denmark. *(line 90)*

Act 1 Scene 5

The Ghost claims he is the spirit of Hamlet's father, and tells that he suffers horribly for his sins, but is forbidden to speak of the appalling terrors he endures. He orders Hamlet to revenge his murder, dismisses the rumour that he was killed by a serpent, and reveals that Claudius murdered him and seduced Gertrude. He expresses disgust that Gertrude now sleeps with his brother. Relating how Claudius poured poison in his ear and so robbed him of life, crown and queen, the Ghost expresses horror at being unprepared for death, dying before he could settle his affairs with God. He implores Hamlet to revenge, but without harming Gertrude. Sensing dawn about to break, he bids Hamlet adieu.

Such a bald summary cannot catch how the Ghost's compelling language creates a dramatic sense of torment, anger and unnatural events. Graphic phrases evoke fear, disgust, and the corruption of bodily decay: 'harrow up thy soul, freeze thy young blood', 'vile and loathsome crust', etc. In Shakespeare's time, audiences would realise that the Ghost suffers terrible agonies in Purgatory, and that realisation would affect their responses. In Roman Catholic theology, Purgatory was the place where sinners who died before confessing had their sins burnt and purged away. Only after that harrowing ordeal could they enter heaven. Protestants in Shakespeare's audience would suspect the Ghost as an evil agent of the Devil, because Protestantism had abolished the notion of Purgatory.

The audience's suspicion of the Ghost would increase further on hearing the Ghost's demand that Hamlet should revenge his father's death. Revenge was forbidden by state and Church alike. The Church considered revenge as a sin for which the revenger's soul was damned, condemning him to suffer everlasting torments after death. The Ghost could therefore be seen as a devilish spirit sent to tempt Hamlet into an action that will result in his suffering for all eternity.

The Ghost mentions the loss of his crown, but seems more concerned with Gertrude than with political affairs. Like Hamlet in Scene 2, he expresses revulsion at the thought of Gertrude's sexual relationship with Claudius ('that incestuous, that adulterate beast'). Hamlet punctuates the Ghost's tale with exclamations and questions, and seems to suggest he already suspects Claudius: 'O my prophetic soul! / My uncle?' He uses a curious image as he promises to revenge:

> Haste me to know't, that I with wings as swift
> As meditation or the thoughts of love
> May sweep to my revenge.   *(lines 29–31)*

The surface meaning is 'as swift as thought', but the notions of 'meditation' and 'love' seem oddly inconsistent with the idea of a speedy revenger. The contradictory nature of the image foreshadows the delays that will occur as Hamlet seeks revenge, and suggests that he will not be a conventional revenge hero. However, after the Ghost leaves, Hamlet seems fully determined on revenge. He has no thoughts about whether the Ghost is good or evil, vowing to remember it and and its command to revenge. He makes clear his feelings towards his mother ('O most pernicious woman!') and towards Claudius ('smiling, damnèd villain!').

When Horatio and Marcellus join him, Hamlet's strange behaviour and language puzzles them: 'These are but wild and whirling words, my lord.' Hamlet claims the Ghost is honest, and insists they swear never to speak of what they have seen. He demands another oath of silence: never to suggest they know the meaning of any mad or grotesque behaviour ('antic disposition') he might in future display. The scene ends with Hamlet setting his personal troubles in a wider, public context, as he reflects on the cruelty of his destiny as revenger who must cure the ills of family and of Denmark:

> The time is out of joint: O cursèd spite,
> That ever I was born to set it right. –   *(lines 189–90)*

Act 1: Critical review

Act 1 poses important questions. A few will be answered as the play unfolds; most will remain open to conflicting interpretations. Is the Ghost genuinely the spirit of Hamlet's father, or an evil spirit sent to trap him? Is it telling the truth in claiming Claudius is a murderer? Does Hamlet love Ophelia? Will Fortinbras invade? Just what is rotten in the state of Denmark?

The act ends with Hamlet seemingly convinced that the Ghost is in truth his father's spirit, even though it has offered him no comfort. Hamlet accepts the Ghost's order to take revenge on Claudius. But Act 1 has already revealed Hamlet's questioning mind, that seeks the truth behind appearances. The uncertainties that he feels, particularly the suspicion that the Ghost may be false, will resurface to hamper his quest for speedy vengeance.

That theme of deceptive appearance recurs throughout the act, and is expressed in the sentence Hamlet writes about Claudius in his notebook: 'That one may smile, and smile, and be a villain'. But in Scene 2, Hamlet's own preference for reality over appearance ('I know not seems') stands in ironic contrast to his intention in Scene 5 'To put an antic disposition on': to pretend to be mad.

Act 1 poses a more general critical question: how much will this play be about personal relationships or about social and political issues? Valid critical interpretations can be offered from each of these perspectives (and others of course, see pages 85–105). For example, a personal approach would analyse character and family relationships, showing Hamlet as a depressed and resentful stepson, full of powerful emotions towards his mother, agonised by her second marriage.

A social and political approach would focus on issues of power and control. On King Hamlet's death, the throne and its power passed to Claudius, not Hamlet, the king's son. Now Denmark is threatened by the army of Young Fortinbras of Norway. Under Claudius' new regime, hostility between states is settled by negotiation, not by personal combat as in the chivalric world of Old Hamlet. But power is still gender-related. Ophelia and Gertrude are subject to male domination, and Gertrude, as seen through the eyes of Hamlet and the Ghost, is the object of male disgust.

Act 2 Scene 1

Polonius instructs Reynaldo to spy on Laertes in Paris. He advises Reynaldo to use devious and indirect methods of enquiry, rather than direct questions, and even to lie about Laertes' behaviour. Polonius' instructions throw more light on his character and hint at the rottenness that pervades Denmark. He is a father willing to use underhand methods to keep watch on his own son. He is also the chief political officer of state, and this is the first example of the surveillance techniques that Polonius uses to maintain control.

Polonius is often played as long-winded and absent-minded. The episode in which his over-detailed advice makes him lose the thread of his argument ('what was I about to say?') is often a moment of high humour in performance. Shakespeare's own audience enjoyed an additional opportunity for laughter: it was a popular rumour that Lord Burghley, Queen Elizabeth's chief minister, had not only given his son a set of precepts, but had sent spies to Paris to keep a watch on him.

But even if Polonius seems a figure of fun, his concern for the need for surveillance is evident. It is a theme that will recur in the next scene, when spies are set on Hamlet. In Elsinore's world of intrigue, even Reynaldo's name is significant. 'Reynard' means 'fox', a creature traditionally thought of as cunning and difficult to detect.

Ophelia enters in some distress: 'I have been so affrighted.' Her description of Hamlet's dishevelled appearance shows that he has begun to enact his intention 'to put an antic disposition on':

> his doublet all unbraced,
> No hat upon his head, his stockings fouled,
> Ungartered, and down-gyvèd to his ankle,
> Pale as his shirt, his knees knocking each other   *(lines 76–9)*

Ophelia's detailed account of Hamlet's strange behaviour is sometimes portrayed in performance, for example in both the film by Zeffirelli and the version by the Russian director Kozintzev. Hamlet's close scrutiny of her face and his deep sigh have been interpreted as reflecting his thoughts on 'Frailty, thy name is woman'. The dramatic function of Ophelia's story is to create suspense and to whet the audience's appetite for Hamlet's next appearance: just how will he look and behave?

Polonius jumps to the conclusion that Hamlet has been driven mad by Ophelia's rejection of his love. He decides to tell all to Claudius. Whether he physically comforts Ophelia is for actors to decide, but how father and daughter behave in performance will add to an audience's perception of character and relationships. However supportively or coldly Polonius behaves, it is significant that he ends this scene, as he did his earlier scene with Ophelia, with a command ('Come'). Ophelia must do as she is ordered.

Act 2 Scene 2

Line numbers identify the nine separate episodes in this long scene:

1–39 Claudius sets Rosencrantz and Guildenstern to spy on Hamlet.

40–85 The ambassadors report on their successful mission to Norway.

86–165 Polonius claims Hamlet loves Ophelia, and proposes to use her in a plot to spy on Hamlet.

166–212 Hamlet insults Polonius.

213–94 Hamlet discovers Rosencrantz and Guildenstern are sent to spy on him.

295–338 Rosencrantz and Guildenstern tell that the players are coming.

339–489 Hamlet welcomes the players and listens to a speech.

490–500 Hamlet asks the First Player to speak new lines at tomorrow night's performance.

501–58 In soliloquy, Hamlet wonders at the contrast between the Player's faked emotion for Hecuba and his own inability to revenge. He plans to use tomorrow's play to find if Claudius really is a murderer.

Claudius has sent for Rosencrantz and Guildenstern, friends and fellow students of Hamlet. His instruction that they discover the cause of Hamlet's strange behaviour echoes the opening of Scene 1, where Polonius gave a similar surveillance order to Reynaldo. Claudius' concern to find out whether some secret reason causes Hamlet's madness ('Whether aught to us unknown afflicts him thus') may suggest that Claudius suspects Hamlet's intentions towards him.

Gertrude promises the two men that they will be royally rewarded. Her language, like Claudius', is polite and entreating, and Rosencrantz and Guildenstern respond with deference. The king's apparent mistaking of the two men's names is a comic moment, perhaps suggesting that they are alike, like Tweedledum and Tweedledee. Some productions present them as identical twins, and play them as indistinguishable and characterless agents of Claudius.

Polonius announces the return of the ambassadors from Norway, and claims to have discovered 'The very cause of Hamlet's lunacy.' He proposes to reveal that cause after the ambassadors have reported. In one of the few moments that Gertrude and Claudius share alone together in the play, Gertrude's uneasy conscience shows she is acutely aware of what really afflicts Hamlet:

> I doubt it is no other but the main:
> His father's death and our o'erhasty marriage.   *(lines 56–7)*

Voltemand reports that the king of Norway has prevented Fortinbras from attacking Denmark, has sent him instead to invade Poland. Claudius seems pleased. His diplomacy has worked. Speaking as a capable and confident ruler he promises to consider granting permission for Fortinbras' army to march through Denmark.

The ambassadors leave, and Polonius embarks on a longwinded explanation of Hamlet's madness. His pompous and circuitous language contrasts ironically with his assertion that 'brevity is the soul of wit', and prompts Gertrude's sharp rebuke:

> More matter with less art.   *(line 95)*

Her criticism has no effect. Polonius carries on playing pedantically with words, usually to the enjoyment of the audience and the irritation of Gertrude. Nearly all productions have Polonius revelling in being the centre of attention. He parades his evidence (Hamlet's letter and poem), comments on poetic style, tells of his instruction to Ophelia to have no contact with Hamlet, and unfolds his conclusion that Hamlet has been driven mad by Ophelia's refusal to see him.

How Claudius reacts throughout Polonius' story varies in each production. Sometimes he shares Gertrude's impatience, sometimes he reacts with amused tolerance. How far Claudius really trusts his chief political officer can often be judged by the way he speaks his four-word reply to Polonius' self-regarding question:

POLONIUS   Hath there been such a time, I'ld fain know that,
     That I have positively said, 'tis so,
     When it proved otherwise?
CLAUDIUS   Not that I know.   *(lines 151–3)*

Claudius' four words can be spoken to convey an impression of trust or of deep suspicion. As such, they are a clue to how a particular performance portrays his character. But Polonius presses on with his claim that he can always discover the truth, however well concealed. He proposes a plot. He will 'loose' Ophelia to Hamlet (the word 'loose', making her sound like a released farmyard animal), and he and Claudius will eavesdrop on their conversation. The plan is yet another example of surveillance (spying on others). It signifies once again this aspect of Denmark's corruption.

There is no stage direction for Hamlet to enter until after Claudius has agreed the plan (line 165). But some directors have Hamlet overhear the plot. Although this can be one more occasion for overhearing, in performance it may reduce the dramatic tension which arises when a character (Hamlet) does not know the intentions of other characters (Polonius and Claudius). If Hamlet overhears, it can also lessen the impact on the audience of their first sight of Hamlet's 'antic disposition'. On stage, Hamlet has appeared in all kinds of ways: in women's clothes, wearing a jester's cap and bells, in pyjamas, crawling, barking, clucking like a hen. In one production, he performed an Egyptian dance.

Hamlet tries to humiliate Polonius throughout their encounter. All his contemptuous insults could be simply nonsense, spoken to confuse Polonius, but each has been given critical significance. For example a 'fishmonger' could mean a brothel keeper, a fisher for information, a person whose daughters had many children, or a lower class person. These meanings, together with some of Hamlet's other insults in the episode, could relate to some aspect of Polonius: Ophelia's father, spymaster, state official, old man. Polonius certainly seems to detect deeper meaning:

Though this be madness, yet there is method in't.   *(line 200)*

Hamlet's jibes at Polonius express disgust with sex, breeding and corruption. He ends their encounter with the scornful 'These tedious old fools!' and greets Rosencrantz and Guildenstern with 'My excellent good friends!'

But after some friendly wordplay involving sexual puns ('her privates we') the mood turns sombre. Hamlet visualises Denmark as a prison and talks of his bad dreams. Guildenstern seizes the opportunity to probe the reason for Hamlet's melancholy, and he interprets dreams as 'ambition'. He perhaps suspects the cause lies in Hamlet's disappointed ambition to become king.

Hamlet grows suspicious of his fellow students, and forces them to admit that they are agents of Claudius: 'we were sent for.' In one of the most remarkable speeches in the play (lines 280–92), Hamlet deliberately misleads his friends with the story they may carry back to Claudius and Gertrude. He says he has lost all his mirth, and the earth and its people, so full of excellence, nobility and beauty, now seem foul and pestilent, and give him no delight. The speech is Shakespeare's eloquent expression of Renaissance views of the infinite potential for good of humankind and the world, combined with contemporary beliefs on the nature of melancholy.

Significantly, Hamlet says nothing about reasons for his melancholy, of which the audience is already aware: his disgust at his mother's marriage, his belief that his father was murdered by Claudius and Ophelia's refusal to see him. He adds a final enigmatic comment, perhaps suggesting that he is not mad at all, and clearly knows the difference between one thing and another, between truth and falsehood:

> I am but mad north-north-west. When the wind is southerly,
> I know a hawk from a handsaw.   *(lines 347–8)*

News of the arrival of the players at Elsinore cheers Hamlet. There may be a hint of menace in Hamlet's 'He that plays the king shall be welcome', but thoughts of King Claudius and the revenge plot seem to disappear. Dramatic pace slackens as Hamlet lists the stock characters in an acting company and eagerly questions why the actors are forced to travel. Shakespeare seems to drift away from the concerns of the play as his characters discuss theatrical conditions in the London of his time (for the 'little eyases' see page 73).

But the episode, seemingly a digression, has relevance to at least three aspects of the play. First, acting embodies Hamlet's theme of appearance and reality, of pretended versus genuine emotions. Second, Hamlet will shortly devise a plan, using the theatrical illusion of a play, to expose Claudius' guilt, and in the soliloquy that ends Act 2 he will reflect on drama as deception. Third, Hamlet uses the discussion on the change in acting fashions to make a barbed comment about Denmark. He notes how easily courtiers who would sneer ('make mouths') at Claudius whilst Hamlet's father lived, now fawn upon Claudius as king, buying his picture for extravagant sums.

Polonius' entrance further displays the politician's self-regarding pomposity as an expert on all matters. As Polonius works up to his climax, Shakespeare may also be seizing the opportunity to satirise the classical rules of drama and the fashion for classifying plays:

> tragical-comical-historical-pastoral, scene individable or poem
> unlimited. *(lines 365–6)*

In response to yet more of Hamlet's taunting, Polonius may touch the audience's emotions as he reveals a very human side to his character: 'I have a daughter that I love passing well.' But Hamlet ridicules that reply too, and sidelines Polonius in order to welcome the players, some of whom he recognises. Hamlet's enthusiasm for players and acting becomes very evident as he jokingly greets individual actors and demands a speech from the First Player. Hamlet says the speech comes from a rarely performed play, too difficult or too refined for the public ('caviary to the general'), but admired by the elite. The speech is almost certainly Shakespeare's own, but it may well be his homage to (or parody of) Christopher Marlowe's tragedy *Dido, Queen of Carthage*, published in 1594. Marlowe's play is written in the same high-flown style, full of exaggerated images. Hamlet says the lines were spoken to Dido by the Greek hero Aeneas. He tells of Pyrrhus, whose father Achilles was killed at the siege of Troy.

Pyrrhus was one of the Greek warriors in the wooden horse ('the ominous horse') which was used to defeat the Trojans. Like Hamlet, he seeks revenge for his slain father. Hamlet himself begins the tale of how the 'rugged' (long-haired) Pyrrhus, covered in blood ('total gules', 'o'er-sizèd with coagulate gore') sought out Priam, King of Troy, to kill him and so avenge his own father's death. Some critics argue that as Hamlet speaks the words, he imagines himself as a bloodthirsty revenger pursuing Claudius:

> With eyes like carbuncles, the hellish Pyrrhus
> Old grandsire Priam seeks –   *(lines 421–2)*

The First Player continues the speech, telling how Pyrrhus finds Priam, pauses for a long moment, then slays him. In some productions Hamlet echoes 'Did nothing' and clearly shows that he is conscious of his own delay in carrying out the act of revenge for his father's murder. It is significant that the two words occupy a single verse line (440), indicating the need for a dramatic pause.

The final part of the Player's speech, after Polonius' interruption, tells of Hecuba, Priam's wife, who wept to see her husband slaughtered. Is Shakespeare making a deliberate dramatic contrast here, setting the deep grief of Hecuba against the brief mourning and unusual speed with which Gertrude remarried after her husband's death? Some critics think he is. They argue that the whole Pyrrhus speech (lines 410–75) can be thought of as Shakespeare writing a commentary on the play, consciously echoing other features of *Hamlet* in addition to the Hecuba/Gertrude contrast:

- the common theme of the death of fathers
- Priam, like Claudius, is responsible for the murder of a father
- Pyrrhus, like Hamlet, wishes to be both king-killer and revenger
- 'strumpet Fortune' echoes Hamlet's exchanges with Rosencrantz and Guildenstern. It also predicts the downfall of a king because of the untrustworthiness of fortune
- the melodramatic style contrasts with the language of *Hamlet*

The speech also serves the dramatic function of placing the players and acting itself at the centre of attention (see also page 72). The actors will shortly play a major part in Hamlet's plot to reveal his uncle's guilt. Furthermore, Hamlet delivers what may be Shakespeare's own estimation of the importance of his profession, claiming that, in drama, actors present the very condition of society itself:

> They are the abstract and brief chronicles of the time.
>   *(lines 481–2)*

The Player ends his speech with tears in his eyes, and it is that display of pretended grief for Hecuba that provokes Hamlet's soliloquy. He wonders at the Player's ability to weep for a fictional character ('And all for nothing? / For Hecuba!'). In reality, Hecuba means nothing to the player and she cares nothing for him. What would the player do if he had 'the motive and the cue for passion' that Hamlet has? The thought provokes Hamlet to reproach himself for apparent cowardice and lack of action when he has real reasons to take revenge. He curses Claudius:

> Bloody, bawdy villain!
> Remorseless, treacherous, lecherous, kindless villain!
> Oh, vengeance! *(lines 532–4)*

But Hamlet, listening to himself as carefully and critically as he listens to others, mocks his emotional outburst: 'Why, what an ass am I!' He realises he must act in some way, sets his brains to work, and thinks what to do ('Hum'). He outlines a plan to test the Ghost's story, and shows much uncertainty about whether the Ghost is honest, or an evil spirit sent to trap him into eternal damnation ('The spirit that I have seen / May be a devil').

A curious feature is that although it seems Hamlet works out what to do during the second half of his soliloquy, he actually began to put his plan into action a little earlier. At lines 490–5 he asked the First Player to present *The Murder of Gonzago* the next night, and to learn some lines that Hamlet will write specially. But even if this is a puzzling aspect of Shakespeare's dramatic construction, Hamlet's intention is clear. The players will perform a play showing a murder similar to how Claudius murdered Old Hamlet. If the watching Claudius reveals his guilt, it will prove that the Ghost has spoken truly:

> The play's the thing
> Wherein I'll catch the conscience of the king. *(lines 557–8)*

Act 2: Critical review

Act 2 appears to resolve political relationships between Denmark and Norway. Claudius seems to have settled the problem of Fortinbras. But most of the other questions raised in Act 1 remain unanswered. Act 2 ends with Hamlet unsure whether the Ghost has told the truth, but still determined on revenge by using the players to discover whether Claudius really is a murderer.

The theme of deceptive appearance recurs in three different forms: madness, theatre and surveillance. In Scene 1 Ophelia reports the first sight of Hamlet's 'antic disposition'. Scene 2 raises the question of whether Hamlet's madness is genuine or pretended. His behaviour is puzzling as he insults Polonius, responds enigmatically to Rosencrantz and Guildenstern, and in soliloquy lashes into a tirade of abuse against himself and Claudius.

The arrival of the players deepens the play's concern with reality and appearance. Hamlet is fascinated by the fact that the First Player apparently experiences profound emotions for Hecuba, a fictional character. Convinced of the power of theatre, he puts into action a plan in which pretence (the staging of a play), will make Claudius reveal the truth or falsity of the Ghost's story.

Act 2 begins and ends with planned surveillance by different methods. It opens with Polonius setting Reynaldo to spy on Laertes. It concludes with Hamlet proposing to watch Claudius ('observe his looks') during the play to detect signs of guilt. Other examples of surveillance occur, seeking to find what lies behind outward appearances. Rosencrantz and Guildenstern are ordered to watch Hamlet to find the real nature of his 'transformation'; Polonius proposes to use Ophelia as bait in a plot to observe Hamlet.

The act provides further insight into 'public' and 'private' aspects of the play. Elsinore is a society full of suspicion, where even old friends cannot be trusted. Although the arrival of the players cheers him, Hamlet still feels deeply troubled and isolated. He is hungry for revenge, but unsure if he knows the truth. His thoughts, emotions, and desire for action struggle with each other, their conflict intensified by the fictional portrayal of a revenging son and a grieving mother: Pyrrhus and Hecuba.

Act 3 Scene 1

Claudius questions Rosencrantz and Guildenstern about Hamlet's 'turbulent and dangerous lunacy'. He seems suspicious that Hamlet merely 'puts on' an act. Guildenstern confirms that suspicion with talk of Hamlet's 'crafty madness'. The two men tell the king of Hamlet's unwillingness to talk about the reasons for his distraction, but they give an inaccurate account of what happened. Contrary to what they say, Hamlet asked many questions and was hardly 'free' in reply to their demands. Their distortions make a small but significant contribution to the atmosphere of deceit that characterises Elsinore.

Hearing of Hamlet's joy at news of the players, Claudius agrees to attend tonight's performance, and urges the two men to encourage Hamlet's interest in the theatre. His words are charged with dramatic irony because only 25 lines earlier Hamlet had resolved to use the play and the power of drama as the very devices with which to test Claudius' guilt. Hamlet intends to disturb the 'content' that Claudius now expresses.

In dramatic contrast to Hamlet's setting his trap for the king, Claudius and Polonius now set their trap for Hamlet. They plan to be legitimate spies ('lawful espials') on Hamlet's meeting with Ophelia. Once again the women are treated as subordinates and are exploited. Gertrude is sent away and Ophelia is instructed on how to behave. How far the women willingly support the spying plot is a matter for each production to decide, but there is a brief opportunity to express female solidarity when Gertrude speaks to Ophelia, hoping her love will restore Hamlet to sanity.

Polonius orders Ophelia to 'Read on this book', as a pretence that will justify her being alone when she meets Hamlet. His instruction prompts him to reflect on the hypocrisy of a pious appearance often covering evil. Hearing that thought, Claudius speaks an aside, exposing his tortured feelings of guilt for his 'deed' hidden behind his deceitful words. He reveals the truth to the audience – he did murder Hamlet's father:

> How smart a lash that speech doth give my conscience!
> The harlot's cheek, beautied with plastering art,
> Is not more ugly to the thing that helps it
> Than is my deed to my most painted word.　　　　*(lines 50–3)*

Before Hamlet speaks his 'To be, or not to be' soliloquy, every production faces very practical staging problems. Just how and where do the two men conceal themselves to spy on Hamlet? Ophelia remains on stage, but where? And what does she do? Just how and when does Hamlet enter? Does he see or hear anything of the plotting? Is he aware from the start that he is being watched?

The soliloquy is perhaps the most famous speech in all Shakespeare. Anywhere in the world, when people are asked what they know of Shakespeare, the line they are most likely to quote is 'To be, or not to be, that is the question'. But even this best-known line is open to a variety of interpretations. Critics argue fiercely over its meaning, and what Hamlet has in mind as he speaks the line. The competing interpretations group into two types:

- Hamlet's own personal dilemma. Here, the major interpretation is that Hamlet is asking himself 'Should I live, or commit suicide?' Another 'personal' interpretation, less frequently offered, is 'Should I kill Claudius?'
- Hamlet is not considering his own situation, but a more general question: 'Is life worth living?' This question of the advantages and disadvantages of human existence, of whether it is better to be unhappy than not to be at all, was a favourite debating topic in Shakespeare's time.

The most widely held interpretation is the first: that Hamlet is thinking about himself, and puzzling whether or not he should commit suicide. Such critics as A C Bradley and John Dover Wilson see the whole soliloquy as an extended reflection on that dilemma. Hamlet first asks himself the question, and wonders whether the most noble course is to suffer all life's hardships or fight against them. He sees death as 'a sleep', but is troubled by what may happen in that sleep of death. He suggests that what stops people committing suicide, in spite of all the oppressions and injustices of life, is fear of the terrors that await the dead. He concludes that such thinking prevents decisive action.

Other critics disagree with the 'suicide' interpretation. They argue that Hamlet is not thinking about what he should do in his own particular situation. He makes no mention of revenge, or of Claudius, Gertrude or the Ghost, and he never uses the personal pronoun 'I', but speaks of 'we' and 'us' and 'who'. This argues for an interpretation that Hamlet is considering a question that applies to everyone: whether, in view of all the afflictions that cause human misery, it is better to have life than not to have it. He is weighing up a human problem, not deciding whether to take action himself (suicide, or killing the king and so bringing about his own death).

Should you believe one of these interpretations over the other? Perhaps it is more appropriate to accept that Hamlet may be simultaneously considering his personal dilemma and the more general question of how to hold life and death in balance. A characteristic of Shakespeare's writing is that a speech can have meaning at more than one level. Here, Hamlet may be setting his practical problem – what action to take – in the context of a more general reflection on why we endure the hardships and injustices of life. He considers both the philosophical issue and how it applies to his own situation.

You can find more on the language of the soliloquy on page 83. At its end, Hamlet's request that Ophelia pray for him can be spoken in a wide variety of tones, from genuine friendship to extreme cynicism. She attempts to return his love-gifts, but he denies ever giving her anything. After an initial protest reminding him of his 'words of so sweet breath' that accompanied the gifts, Ophelia is reduced to brief responses to Hamlet's increasingly bitter taunts. In some productions, the hidden Polonius or Claudius makes a noise that reveals their presence to Hamlet, causing him to be suspicious of Ophelia:

Ha, ha, are you honest? *(line 103)*

He suspects that, like Rosencrantz and Guildenstern, Ophelia is an agent of Claudius' plot, and that the meeting is an arranged trick. That sense of yet another betrayal, together with a desire to exhibit yet more aspects of his 'antic disposition' to Claudius may explain Hamlet's virulent verbal abuse of Ophelia. He says that he once loved her, then denies it, accuses himself of all kinds of faults, and orders her to a 'nunnery'. There is considerable ambiguity in the command: for Elizabethans a nunnery was both a convent and a slang term for a brothel. Hamlet might be pleading with her to become a nun, and so avoid breeding sinners, or he may be condemning her as a whore.

When Ophelia tells him a direct lie, claiming her father is at home, the intensity of Hamlet's abuse increases. He reviles her, and wishes her ill. In tones of extreme sexual disgust he scapegoats her, slandering all women as he accuses them of treacherously exploiting their sex as bait to trap men. His claim that such deceit 'hath made me mad' may be a misleading clue intended for Claudius' ear. In many productions Hamlet's cry that 'all but one shall live' is often unambiguously directed at the hidden king.

Hamlet leaves, repeating his order to Ophelia 'To a nunnery, go.' Her sorrowing lament paints a picture of an ideal prince fallen from excellence into madness:

> Oh what a noble mind is here o'erthrown!
> The courtier's, soldier's, scholar's, eye, tongue, sword,
> Th'expectancy and rose of the fair state,
> The glass of fashion and the mould of form,
> Th'observed of all observers, quite, quite down   *(lines 144–8)*

Ophelia's lines are often regarded as an example of Shakespeare's genius in writing lyrical, metaphorical verse. But her speech is not universally admired. The critic Frank Kermode comments on the 'rather dull doublets' in ten of the twelve lines (for 'doubling' see pages 78–9). A more radical criticism would point out that her speech merely encapsulates the traditional flattering descriptions of royalty, used to create a false public image of a ruler, and that the audience has seen little evidence of most of those qualities in Hamlet.

But Ophelia clearly feels 'deject and wretched'. She has been emotionally devastated by Hamlet's verbal assaults, and Polonius' comment sounds callous and unfeeling: 'You need not tell us what Lord Hamlet said, / We heard it all.' The two men's cold indifference to Ophelia's suffering is often emphasised on stage. Claudius is dismissive of the notion that love has caused Hamlet's strange behaviour. Suspecting danger, he plans to send Hamlet to England. Polonius proposes yet more spying, saying he will watch Hamlet's meeting with Gertrude. Claudius agrees, and his final line expresses the need for surveillance in the state:

> Madness in great ones must not unwatched go.   *(line 182)*

Act 3 Scene 2

Hamlet lectures the players on how to act. They may listen with respect or with barely concealed amusement and contempt at being instructed by a mere amateur, even if he is a prince. In some productions, Hamlet's opening words ('Speak the speech') clearly refer to the lines he has specially written for the play before the king: he holds a sheet of paper and has been coaching the player on how to speak them.

Hamlet urges moderation in acting style, even in passionate speeches. His advice stands in ironic contrast to his violent, unrestrained words to Ophelia in the previous scene. Some people claim they can detect Shakespeare's own voice in the speech. They say he is criticising the overacting of his contemporaries, clowns who ad-lib or laugh at their own jokes, and audiences who enjoy that fooling rather than the play itself. Whether or not that is true, two aspects of Hamlet's advice have particular relevance to *Hamlet* and to the nature of theatre itself. He defines 'the purpose of playing' as

> to hold as 'twere the mirror up to nature; to show virtue her
> own feature, scorn her own image, and the very age and body
> of the time his form and pressure. *(lines 18–20)*

Hamlet's definition has become generally accepted as a crucial purpose of theatre. It should mirror and critically comment on the times, showing society's values, practices and beliefs as they really are. This 'purpose of playing' implies that a student of *Hamlet* needs to identify the nature of Hamlet's Denmark, and to understand in what ways it reflects the society of Shakespeare's time and of our own.

Hamlet's abrupt dismissal of Rosencrantz and Guildenstern provides a dramatic contrast to his warm praise for Horatio: false friends are distinguished from a true friend. His generous description of Horatio provides yet another contrast. Describing him as a man who suffers without complaint, and is not trapped by his emotions ('passion's slave'), Hamlet contrasts Horatio's well-balanced temperament with his own rapidly swinging moods. Significantly, Hamlet ends with yet another surveillance plot: Horatio must watch Claudius' reaction to the play. If the king does not show guilt, then the Ghost's accusation is false.

The court assembles with much ceremony to watch the play. Hamlet mockingly puns on what Claudius and Polonius say to him, and subjects Ophelia to crude sexual innuendo. He comments bitterly on Gertrude's appearance:

> look you how cheerfully my mother looks, and my father died
> within's two hours   *(lines 112–13)*

Ophelia's correction 'Nay, 'tis twice two months my lord', prompts him to more bitter words on his mother's hasty second marriage:

> O heavens! die two months ago, and not forgotten yet?
>   *(line 116)*

In Elizabethan drama, a dumb show often preceded the play, summarising the action. The players' dumb show acts out the murder of a sleeping king by a man who steals both his crown and his queen. It is a mirror image of what Claudius did to his brother, and critics have puzzled over why Claudius does not react to seeing his crime so publicly presented. John Dover Wilson's book *What Happens in Hamlet* was written in response to this problem. Dover Wilson's solution is simple: Claudius does not watch the dumb show but is distracted by attention to Gertrude. But an alternative explanation is that Claudius' lack of response reveals how skilled he is at concealing his true feelings.

The play then repeats the story. In highly formal language the Player King tells of his thirty years of loving and holy marriage. In equally elaborate and artificial rhyming verse the Player Queen expresses worries about his health, but vows not to marry again. The Player King replies that such vows are often broken, because time makes us forget our intentions, however strong. Once again the Player Queen swears she will never remarry (these may be the lines Hamlet has written, but no one knows for sure). Hamlet uses her repeated vow to test his mother (who must surely recognise the parody of her own remarriage). Every actress playing Gertrude has to decide just how far they will reveal or conceal their feelings in their one-line reply:

HAMLET Madam, how like you this play?
GERTRUDE The lady doth protest too much methinks. *(lines 210–11)*

After subjecting Ophelia to yet more crude sexual innuendo, Hamlet uses the language of conventional revenge tragedy as he orders Lucianus, the murderer, to act ('the croaking raven doth bellow for revenge'). The sight of the poison being poured into the sleeping king's ears, together with Hamlet's taunt 'You shall see anon how the murderer gets the love of Gonzago's wife', provokes Claudius to respond. He leaves, calling for light, and the play abruptly ends. Just how Claudius' departure is staged varies enormously. In some productions he is agitated and terrified, in others calm and dignified. In the Russian film he mockingly claps the performance; in one stage production he contemptuously tipped the players as he left.

However Claudius reacts, Hamlet clearly feels his plan has succeeded, and he jokes delightedly with Horatio. He believes that the Ghost has told the truth and that Claudius has revealed his guilt. In mocking exchanges with Rosencrantz and Guildenstern, Hamlet shows their friendship is ended. He taunts Guildenstern, inviting him to play on a recorder. When Guildenstern denies he has any ability, Hamlet uses an extended musical metaphor as he launches into a bitter denunciation:

> Why look you now how unworthy a thing you make of me.
> You would play upon me, you would seem to know my stops,
> you would pluck out the heart of my mystery, you would
> sound me from my lowest note to the top of my compass ...
> *(lines 329–32)*

Hamlet refuses to be treated as a mere musical instrument, to be made to say anything at someone else's wish. He demonstrates how someone can be made to pipe to another's tune in his exchange with Polonius, making him agree with improbable comparisons of a cloud to a camel, a weasel and a whale. He ends the scene with a soliloquy that uses the melodramatic stock imagery of the traditional revenger of Elizabethan drama 'Now could I drink hot blood'. As he leaves to meet Gertrude, he vows to upbraid her, but not harm her:

> I will speak daggers to her but use none.   *(line 357)*

Act 3 Scene 3

Claudius briefs Rosencrantz and Guildenstern to prepare to take Hamlet to England, because he presents a dangerous threat. The two men flatter the king. Their words express the official ideology of Tudor England that everything and everybody in the state depend upon the monarch. As they picture the disasters which follow from the fall of a king, their flattery is unwittingly ironic: Claudius has himself killed the legitimate king. Polonius also flatters Claudius as he reports his plan to spy on Hamlet and Gertrude. The plan was hatched by Polonius, but he flatteringly gives the king credit for suggesting it ('And as you said, and wisely was it said').

In his soliloquy, Claudius admits his guilt ('Oh my offence is rank, it smells to heaven'). He hopes for divine mercy for his brother's murder, but he knows that pardon is impossible while he retains the fruits of his crime: 'My crown, mine own ambition, and my queen.' He knows that although he might escape judgement and punishment on earth, there is no escape for him in heaven, except by gaining God's forgiveness through prayer and true repentance. Though he feels he is in no state to pray or repent, he calls on angels to help, and kneels to pray. Frank Kermode judges Claudius' conscience-stricken soliloquy as signalling 'the fuller maturity of Shakespeare's verse':

> Here is a man suffering from his thought, working out his
> violent emotion in violent, immediate language, subjected to
> the pressure and slippage of bold, even anguished, metaphor
> … Here we have the energy, the flurries of oblique association,
> that characterise Shakespeare at his best.

Hamlet enters, and for a moment his thoughts and actions echo Pyrrhus about to slaughter Priam (see Act 2 Scene 2, lines 426–50). But Hamlet refrains from killing Claudius because the king is praying. To kill him at prayer would be to send Claudius' soul to heaven. Hamlet reflects that his own father had been killed at a moment when he was unprepared for heaven, not having confessed his sins, and so condemned to suffering after death. Hamlet resolves to kill Claudius at a more sinful moment, and thus damn him to hell.

Critics have argued fiercely over Hamlet's delay in killing Claudius. Some, notably Doctor Johnson, find his reason (to ensure that Claudius suffers eternally) morally revolting. Others argue that

Hamlet is finding an excuse to delay, or simply not telling the truth. He just cannot kill a man in cold blood because he is not a hard-hearted traditional revenger. But whatever causes him to procrastinate, there is dramatic irony in Claudius' final couplet. It reveals that Hamlet may have caught the conscience of the king, but that he was deceived by appearance. Claudius only looked as if he was praying. His efforts to contact God were unsuccessful:

> My words fly up, my thoughts remain below.
> Words without thoughts never to heaven go.　　　*(lines 97–8)*

Act 3 Scene 4

The scene takes place in Gertrude's closet, which for Elizabethans meant a private room. But Olivier's film and many stage productions set it in Gertrude's bedroom. This setting heightens the Freudian interpretation that Hamlet has an Oedipus complex, which implies that Hamlet secretly wishes to kill his father and take his place in his mother's bed. Such desires, the Freudians argue, cause Hamlet's delay in revenging his father's murder.

Polonius finally pays the price for eavesdropping. He advises Gertrude to speak sharply to her son, then hides behind the arras (curtain). Hamlet vehemently criticises his mother, making her fear for her life. Her alarm prompts Polonius to call for help, and Hamlet, in stark contrast to his delay a few minutes earlier, immediately responds, suspecting it is Claudius he hears. He thrusts his sword through the arras, killing Polonius. Gertrude's four-word response to Hamlet's accusation is often interpreted as her dawning recognition that her first husband was murdered, perhaps by her second:

HAMLET A bloody deed? Almost as bad, good mother,

　　As kill a king and marry with his brother.
GERTRUDE As kill a king?　　　　　　　　　　*(lines 28–30)*

Hamlet dismisses the dead Polonius as a meddling fool, and embarks on a diatribe against his mother, determined to stir her conscience. He accuses her of shamelessly defiling true love and marriage, making heaven itself blush with shame. He compares his father with Claudius ('Look here upon this picture, and on this'), setting the good man against the bad. He berates Gertrude for not seeing the difference, and deplores her inability to control her sexual desires.

His words strike Gertrude's conscience, and she admits seeing 'black and grainèd spots' upon her soul. But Hamlet continues his denunciation. He works himself up to an expression of extreme disgust at Gertrude's sexuality:

> Nay, but to live
> In the rank sweat of an enseamèd bed,
> Stewed in corruption, honeying and making love
> Over the nasty sty.   *(lines 91–4)*

As Hamlet reviles Claudius and his mother pleads with him to stop, the Ghost enters. It reminds Hamlet of his 'almost blunted purpose' to revenge, and urges him to comfort Gertrude who, amazed at Hamlet's words and actions, thinks him mad. Gertrude's inability to see the Ghost is sometimes interpreted as signifying her moral blindness.

Although Hamlet urges his mother to confess and repent, he seems more obsessed with Gertrude's sexual relationship with Claudius. He pleads with her not to sleep with the king tonight. His claim to be heaven's agent in killing Polonius ('I must be their scourge and minister') recalls his earlier lament 'The time is out of joint' and that he was 'born to set it right'. That notion that he is divinely appointed to punish sin may lie behind his excuse for his harsh treatment of his mother:

> I must be cruel only to be kind;   *(line 179)*

Urging Gertrude not to reveal his pretended madness to 'the bloat king' Claudius during their love-making, Hamlet prepares to leave. She promises to keep silent, and Hamlet reveals he plans to kill his untrustworthy friends Rosencrantz and Guildenstern: 'I will delve one yard below their mines / And blow them at the moon.' With a final insulting description of Polonius as 'a foolish prating knave', he crudely expresses his intention to hide the body of the dead counsellor:

> I'll lug the guts into the neighbour room.   *(line 213)*

Act 3: Critical review

Hamlet's moods continue to fluctuate violently. His soliloquy at the end of Act 2 ended exultantly with an emphatic decision to trap Claudius by means of a play. That mood now contrasts strikingly with his 'To be or not to be' soliloquy. His emotional state seems once again to resemble the despair and disillusion of his first soliloquy in Act 1 ('O that this too too solid flesh would melt').

But Hamlet's dejection gives way to wildly veering moods and actions in each of the four scenes of Act 3. His manic-depressive state has cruel consequences. The two women endure Hamlet's sexual disgust. Ophelia is subjected to harsh invective and humiliation, and Gertrude is reviled as Hamlet returns obsessively to her sexuality. Polonius is abruptly killed and dismissed as 'knave' and 'guts'.

Plot and counterplot flourish. Hamlet is spied upon, and in turn exposes Claudius' guilt through the play-within-a-play. His title for the play, 'The Mousetrap', is significantly prophetic. It succeeds in its purpose to 'catch the conscience of the king'. Claudius proposes to send his dangerous nephew to England, guarded by Rosencrantz and Guildenstern, but Hamlet has ominous intentions for his two schoolfellows, predicting he will 'blow them at the moon.'

The play's preoccupation with appearance and reality is much in evidence. In Scene 1 Claudius admits that the 'plastering art' of the harlot resembles the way he too covers corruption behind a false mask. In the same scene Hamlet reviles women's 'paintings', claiming such deceit causes his madness. In the closet scene the supernatural world again intrudes, in the Ghost's brief appearance. But significantly, he is invisible to Gertrude.

Ironic emphasis is given to the theatre metaphor that pervades the play. Hamlet advises the players that an audience's attention should not be distracted from 'some necessary question of the play', that is, from a crucial theme or issue which recurs in different ways throughout the play. In Hamlet, one such 'necessary question' is revenge. Hamlet's delay in taking his revenge can be interpreted as his own continued refusal to consider that 'necessary question'. But his rash action in slaying Polonius will give revenge added impulse, when in Act 4 Laertes returns to Elsinore to exact vengeance.

Act 4 Scene 1

There is usually only a slight pause between the end of Act 3 and the opening of this scene. Gertrude remains on stage to be found, sobbing and shuddering, by Claudius. Hearing that Hamlet has killed Polonius, Claudius expresses no regret for his dead counsellor, but fears that he himself might have been the victim:

> It had been so with us had we been there.   *(line 13)*

This is the only time in the play that Claudius and Gertrude are alone together, and it is significant that both lie to each other. Claudius says that although Hamlet is a threat to everyone, he loves him. Gertrude, keeping her promise to Hamlet, deceives Claudius, telling him that Hamlet is mad and that he weeps for killing Polonius. Some productions use these mutual deceptions to show the beginning of a rift between the king and queen, by having Gertrude refusing to respond to any of Claudius' three commands to 'come away'.

Claudius decides to exile Hamlet from Denmark the very next morning. He orders Rosencrantz and Guildenstern to find Hamlet and to take Polonius' body to the chapel. His instinct for self-preservation is again seen as he hopes he can avoid slanderous accusations. In this short scene neither Gertrude nor Claudius tell each other the details of the emotional turmoil they have so recently experienced, but Claudius' final line reveals his deeply troubled mind:

> My soul is full of discord and dismay.   *(line 45)*

Act 4 Scene 2

Hamlet has just hidden Polonius' body ('Safely stowed'). Different performances have presented Hamlet very differently in this scene. In one, he was discovered washing his bloody clothes. In the Russian film he feigns sleep. But all productions attempt to bring out both the humour of the scene and Hamlet's contempt for Rosencrantz ('a sponge') and the king ('an ape', 'nothing'). In many productions Hamlet runs away as he speaks the final line, chased by the two courtiers:

> Hide fox, and all after!   *(line 27)*

Act 4 Scene 3

Claudius seems once again the capable monarch as he explains he cannot punish Hamlet severely because Hamlet is popular in Denmark. But Claudius betrays his low opinion of the people he governs, calling them 'the distracted multitude' (the muddle-headed many). Like a modern spin-doctor concerned for public opinion, Claudius says he must make his action in exiling Hamlet seem 'smooth and even'.

Hamlet is brought in under guard, but taunts the king in everything he says:

CLAUDIUS Now Hamlet, where's Polonius?

HAMLET At supper.

CLAUDIUS At supper? Where?

HAMLET Not where he eats, but where he is eaten. A certain
    convocation of politic worms are e'en at him.   *(lines 16–20)*

Hamlet puns on the Diet ('convocation') of Worms (a town in Germany) where in 1521 the Protestant Martin Luther defended his anti-papal views. The worms are 'politic' because they infiltrate the dead body just as Polonius had insinuated his way into the state and Hamlet's privacy. Hamlet continues to stress corruption, decay and the levelling nature of death as he mockingly tells how a king may go 'a progress' (a royal journey) through the guts of a beggar. Hamlet's sardonic humour culminates in his ironic remark as Claudius despatches attendants to bring Polonius' body: 'He will stay till you come.'

Claudius, pretending he has Hamlet's welfare in mind, tells Hamlet that a ship and attendants wait to take him to England. Hamlet's 'Farewell dear mother' again taunts the king, but equally reveals Hamlet's obsession with his mother's sexual relationship with Claudius. Finally alone on stage, Claudius drops his mask and, comparing Hamlet to a fever, reveals he has written letters ordering Hamlet's immediate execution in England:

>   Do it England,
> For like the hectic in my blood he rages,
> And thou must cure me.   *(lines 61–3)*

Act 4 Scene 4

Fortinbras sends a captain to ask Claudius for permission for his Norwegian army to pass through Danish territory. In the Folio version of the play (see page 56) the rest of the scene does not appear. It is thought that Shakespeare himself might have cut what follows, perhaps to shorten the play for touring. The films of Olivier and Zeffirelli, and stage productions which omit Fortinbras, cut the whole scene. But Hamlet's final soliloquy, and the similarity and difference between him and Fortinbras (both revengeful sons; one active, the other inactive) can help the audience and reader gain a more complete understanding of the play.

The Captain tells Hamlet that the army will fight for a tiny, unprofitable part of Poland. Hamlet reflects on the sickness of an apparently healthy society ('th'impostume of much wealth and peace') in which thousands will die in a battle over such a 'straw' (trivial matter). The thought prompts his final soliloquy reproaching himself for delay in revenging his father's death. Everything he encounters prompts him to take vengeance:

> How all occasions do inform against me,
> And spur my dull revenge!   *(lines 32–3)*

He reflects that God has given humans intelligence to use, and that capacity for making reasoned moral decisions is what separates humans from animals. But something prevents Hamlet from action even though he knows he must revenge. Is it forgetfulness, or too much thinking, or cowardice? Hamlet does not know. But he deludes himself about his situation:

> Sith I have cause, and will, and strength, and means
> To do't.   *(lines 45–6)*

He does have the cause (his father's murder), but so far he has lacked the will to put a revenge plan into action. More obviously, at this moment, a prisoner under guard being escorted to exile, he signally lacks both power and resources ('strength' and 'means') to revenge. But the sight of 20,000 men going to their deaths over a trivial cause ('an egg-shell') teaches him that honour must always be defended. Just as with all his soliloquies Hamlet had used some incident or situation to explore the contradictions facing him, now the encounter with Fortinbras' army spurs Hamlet to speed his revenge:

> Oh from this time forth,
> My thoughts be bloody or be nothing worth.   *(lines 65–6)*

Act 4 Scene 5

The scene shifts back to Elsinore. Gertrude agrees to admit Ophelia, but in an aside she candidly expresses her 'sick soul', revealing a sense of guilt and misgivings about the future. Some critics take her aside to imply that she shares Claudius' secret and is complicit in her first husband's murder. Others argue that it indicates the guilty conscience for the sexual 'sin' that Hamlet sees in her.

The stage direction in the First Quarto (see page 55) reads 'Enter Ophelia playing on a lute, and her hair down singing'. The Second Quarto reads 'Enter Ophelia, distracted'. Her mental and emotional derangement has been acted in many ways, dreamily trance-like or bitterly angry are only two possibilities. In Shakespeare's time it was customary for madness in women to be marked by a long wig of loose hair. In many recent productions she has worn an article of Polonius' clothing. That visual sign can add poignancy to the fragments of popular ballads she sings.

The first song clearly recalls the death of her father. But it has also been interpreted as referring to Ophelia's fantasies about Hamlet and the death of their love, and about Gertrude. In some productions Gertrude flinches at the opening two lines, as if reminded of her first husband:

> How should I your true love know
> From another one?   *(lines 23–4)*

Ophelia's enigmatic 'They say the owl was a baker's daughter' may have meaning in the traditional association of owls with death, and bakers' daughters with lust. Claudius attributes her words to grief for her father, but they may be yet another of Shakespeare's ways of showing that distinguishing between reality and appearance is no easy matter. Ophelia, genuinely deranged unlike Hamlet, also has 'method' in her 'madness'.

Ophelia's next song tells of the loss of virginity, betrayed love and men's sexual duplicity. 'Tomorrow is Saint Valentine's day' has been variously interpreted as her seduction by Hamlet, or Gertrude's seduction by Claudius. But her final prose speech seems to be unequivocally about Polonius' death, and her warning 'My brother shall know of it' turns into reality in only a few minutes' time when Laertes appears, seeking revenge.

Claudius again attributes Ophelia's madness solely to grief for her father, then reflects that sorrows never come alone ('When sorrows come, they come not single spies, / But in battalions'). He catalogues the troubles that beset him: Polonius killed, Hamlet exiled, the citizens restless and suspicious, the secret burial of Polonius, Ophelia mad and Laertes a prey to rumour-mongers ('buzzers') among the people.

Shakespeare now stages that final, very political 'sorrow'. A messenger reports that Laertes and an angry mob are coming, and the 'rabble' proclaim Laertes should be king. The news provokes Gertrude's seemingly uncharacteristic outburst, condemning the people who dare question Claudius' authority: 'Oh this is counter, you false Danish dogs!' The violently enraged Laertes commands Claudius to produce Polonius. Gertrude restrains him, but Claudius orders her to let him go, and claims that he is protected by the divine aura of kingship. God himself prevents harm coming to a monarch:

> There's such divinity doth hedge a king
> That treason can but peep to what it would,
> Acts little of his will.   *(lines 124–6)*

Learning of his father's death, Laertes becomes the fourth revenger in the play (with Fortinbras, Pyrrhus and Hamlet). His language is that of the traditional revenger of Elizabethan tragedy:

> To hell allegiance, vows to the blackest devil,
> Conscience and grace to the profoundest pit!   *(lines 131–2)*

Claudius' promise to prove his innocence for Polonius' death is interrupted by Ophelia's second appearance. Laertes did not know of Ophelia's descent into madness, and the sight of her deranged state appals him, but moves him even more strongly to revenge. Ophelia sings again of death, and talks of her father's death. The flowers and herbs she distributes recall a custom in which mourners at a funeral were handed flowers to strew on the grave. They also held special symbolic significance in Elizabethan folklore: rosemary for remembrance, fennel for flatterers, columbines for unfaithfulness, rue for regret and repentance, daisies for deception in love, violets for faithfulness. In rehearsal, actors discuss who should be given which plant, and how the character should react to its special significance. For example, if Laertes is given rosemary, how does he respond?

Ophelia's final song seems clearly to be about her father's death. The pathos of what Laertes sees and hears increases his grief. Claudius, probably seeing the opportunity to exploit the situation to his own advantage, sympathises with Laertes and makes him an offer: if Claudius proves to blame, Laertes can be king. If not, Claudius will help Laertes find justice and revenge for his father's death. Each production must decide whether Gertrude, silent from line 128, hears the words that threaten her son's life:

> And where th'offence is, let the great axe fall.   *(line 213)*

Act 4 Scene 6

One production solved the problem of why Horatio reads the letter aloud by having the sailors hold the letter in front of him. He turned it upside down (showing they cannot read) and began to read it silently. The sailors threatened him, obviously wanting to hear how the letter affected them. It tells that Hamlet was captured in a sea battle, but has done a deal with the pirates and returned to Denmark. The scene confirms Hamlet's warm relationship with Horatio, shows that Claudius' 'execution' plot has failed, tells of dramatic events that Shakespeare chose not to stage, and suggests, by the purposeful tone of the letter, that Hamlet is now determined on action.

Act 4 Scene 7

The previous 'letter' scene has given time for Claudius to explain to .Laertes how Polonius was killed, and that Hamlet tried to kill him too. Now he explains that he did not punish Hamlet for two reasons: love of Gertrude, and Hamlet's popularity with the people of Denmark. Significantly, he makes no mention of Hamlet's madness. He hints that he has ordered Hamlet's death, but is then much puzzled by the letter from Hamlet telling of his return.

Laertes welcomes the chance to gain revenge, and Claudius, realising his 'execution in England' plot has failed, seizes the opportunity: 'Will you be ruled by me?' Claudius had begun by calming Laertes; he now sees the chance to use him to kill Hamlet. The powerfully focused dialogue that follows is sometimes called the 'temptation scene' as Claudius corrupts Laertes to be his agent in another murderous plot.

Claudius cunningly works by indirection. He says that Hamlet envies Laertes, but delays naming the reason for that envy. He talks instead of a Frenchman, Lamord, who praised Laertes' swordsmanship. This episode seems a long digression, but it has dramatic value in displaying more of Claudius' devious character, and expanding the horizons of the play as it hints at a past war with France and a Renaissance world of chivalry. Even Lamord's name may be symbolic, sounding like the French *la mort* – death.

Laertes, probably impatient, asks what is the point of Claudius' words, and the king now uses emotional blackmail. Echoing the Player King's speech, Claudius talks of how love fades with time, and implies that Laertes' love for his father may also fade. The trick succeeds as Laertes blurts out what he is willing to do to exact his revenge on Hamlet:

> To cut his throat i'th'church.   *(line 125)*

Claudius, unaware of the dramatic irony of Laertes' words (his life has recently been spared as he knelt to pray) plans a fencing match in which one of the swords will not be blunted. Laertes offers to poison the sharpened point of the blade, and Claudius, who has already poisoned one man, proposes poisoning Hamlet's drink. Elizabethan audiences, watching the two men planning more poisoning, may well have experienced feelings of abhorrence. Poisoning was considered an especially villainous crime, the practice of evil foreigners.

Gertrude's report of Ophelia's death changes the mood of the scene. Her lyrical description has been a source of inspiration for artists (notably the Victorian painter Millais). But her speech, much admired by some, has evoked very different critical responses. Some criticise the language as artificial; they see it as unrealistically fanciful, prettified and romantic. Others ask a practical question: why did she not act to save Ophelia? They claim Gertrude sounds uncharacteristically more like a dispassionate observer than a compassionate woman. Others wonder if she is telling the truth, and whether Ophelia's death was not an accident but suicide.

Critics who admire and justify the speech make some of the following points:

- Shakespeare may be recalling an actual drowning near Stratford-upon-Avon in 1579.
- Gertrude is softening the horror to Laertes, to make Ophelia's death more acceptable.
- The images of nature contrast with the bestial images used by Hamlet, and are rich in literary associations:
  - the willow was thought of as a 'sad tree' from which rejected lovers made mourning garlands;
  - the various flowers signify weeping, death and love, and reflect Shakespeare's use of flowers elsewhere in the play;
  - the 'weeping brook' is an example of personification and the pathetic fallacy (the poetic assumption that nature has human emotions).
- Ophelia's chanting of 'lauds' (Christian hymns) contrasts with Laertes' unchristian desire for revenge. Her innocence balances his fall from grace by readily consenting to Claudius' devious plot.
- The supremely imaginative nature of the speech is appropriate to the dramatic qualities of the play.

The effect of Gertrude's story on Laertes suggests he is more than a bloodthirsty revenger. He unsuccessfully fights back tears, unable to control his feelings of grief for his sister. The scene ends with Claudius bidding Gertrude twice to 'follow' (does she?), and characteristically telling yet another lie:

How much I had to do to calm his rage! *(line 192)*

Act 4: Critical review

Act 4 once again sets the play in its political context. In Scene 3 Claudius is concerned that the people of Denmark look favourably on his actions. The audience is reminded that England, recently defeated in a bloody battle, is Denmark's client state, and must instantly perform King Claudius' order to execute Hamlet. Scene 4 further expands the play's political horizons as it moves outside Elsinore and portrays the army of Norway marching to invade Poland.

In Scene 5 Claudius' words express the official ideology of the Tudor and Jacobean state: 'There's such divinity doth hedge a king'. The doctrine of the divine right of kings, that the monarch was God's representative on earth, was a belief that 40 years after Shakespeare wrote *Hamlet* would result in the English Civil War and the beheading of King Charles I. By putting the words in the mouth of the devious Claudius, Shakespeare may be inviting a subversive attitude to the notion that kings are divinely appointed by God.

Shakespeare also suggests how the ordinary people of Denmark contribute to political instability. In Scene 5 Claudius is concerned about public reaction to Polonius' death, and Horatio fears that Ophelia's strange behaviour 'may strew / Dangerous conjectures in ill-breeding minds'. But the ordinary people make only the briefest of appearances. They shout for Laertes to be king, and break down the doors of the palace, but they readily obey Laertes' command to leave.

In such ways, Act 4 underlines the political context of the play. But it also keeps the focus squarely upon the feelings and thoughts of individuals. Earlier in the play, Hamlet had been prompted to reproach himself for his delay by the sight of the First Player's tears for Hecuba. Now another illusion (Fortinbras' soldiers prepared to die for nothing other than a false conception of honour) produces a similar self-reproach. He declares his compelling reasons for revenge, 'a father killed, a mother stained', and determines to act.

This act shows the consequences of Hamlet's killing of Polonius. Laertes turns into another of the play's revengers and Ophelia is driven into madness. This domestic tragedy of father, son and daughter gives Claudius his opportunity. He craftily seduces Laertes to be his instrument to murder Hamlet.

Act 5 Scene 1

Shakespeare now stages an audacious change of mood, scene and character. Comedy in a graveyard is suddenly juxtaposed with the sombre atmosphere of the preceding scene. The common people of Denmark are given a powerful voice as the two Gravediggers discuss Ophelia's death. In Shakespeare's time, and indeed up to the twentieth century, suicides were refused burial in a churchyard, but the Gravediggers believe Ophelia committed suicide. They think she is being allowed a Christian burial because of her high rank, and they question such social privilege:

> If this had not been a gentlewoman, she should have been
> buried out o' Christian burial.   *(lines 20–1)*

Today, the Gravediggers' mangling of the language can be funny in its own right, but Shakespeare's audiences would recognise references to contemporary events and issues. The talk of the man going to the water and the three parts of an act recalls familiar gossip about a famous Elizabethan law case. The suicide of Sir James Hales gave rise to much legal wrangling over the three parts of an action and whether Sir James went to the water or whether it came to him.

In the eighteenth and nineteenth centuries, this intrusion of comedy shocked many admirers of the play. They condemned Shakespeare's artistry, because they believed that the 'high' tone of tragedy should be kept quite separate from comedy or lower class characters. Many productions, notably those of David Garrick in the eighteenth century, omitted the Gravediggers altogether, feeling they lowered the tone of the play.

But Shakespeare here, as in all his other tragedies, uses comedy and low-status characters for more than comic relief. The scene increases dramatic effect by providing alternative perspectives. Central concerns of the play are expressed from the viewpoint of the ordinary people of Denmark as the Gravedigger puzzles his mate with a riddle, sings as he digs, then jokes with Hamlet.

Every production considers whether it should present Hamlet as changed, in appearance and character, since the audience's last sight of him. Has experience made him more relaxed and tranquil? But however he is portrayed, Hamlet still displays the trait that has characterised him throughout the play: whatever he sees sets him thinking. He comments on the skulls the Gravedigger throws out. His mention of Cain may be a subtle reminder of Claudius (in the Bible, Cain kills his brother Abel). He speculates on the levelling effect of death: the skulls of politicians, courtiers and lawyers all look alike. Death is no respecter of persons. The bones of a flattering courtier end up as mere skittles, and in spite of a lawyer's many legal documents entitling him to land, death is the only end: all anyone finishes up with is the six feet of a grave.

The Gravedigger's playing and punning with language prompts Hamlet to reflect on the way peasants imitate courtiers. The exchange revealing that Hamlet is aged thirty contains a joke that is as much enjoyed today as it was in Shakespeare's time. Asked why the mad Hamlet has been sent to England, the Gravedigger replies that even if Hamlet doesn't recover his wits there, it won't matter because:

> There the men are as mad as he. *(line 130)*

The Elizabethans' fascination with the decay of the human body after death is evident in the Gravedigger's reply to Hamlet's question 'How long will a man lie i'th'earth ere he rot?' The skull the Gravedigger hands up from the grave affects Hamlet deeply. This is a much-loved companion of his childhood, the jester Yorick, whose wit and vitality entertained the whole court. The image and words of Hamlet contemplating Yorick's skull are known worldwide, but after his 'Alas poor Yorick!' he expresses disgust for the physical corruption that inevitably follows death. That sense of corruption and disgust brings his mother (or all women) to mind, together with his feelings about female deceit. He mordantly instructs the skull:

> Now get you to my lady's chamber, and tell her, let her paint
> an inch thick, to this favour she must come. Make her laugh at
> that. *(lines 163–5)*

His words recall his earlier disgust at women's 'paintings', but they may also be an uncomfortable reminder of Queen Elizabeth. For the last years of her reign she was highly made up. A report in 1600 claimed her to be painted 'in some places near half an inch thick'. Hamlet jokingly reasons and rhymes that death turns great conquerors like Alexander the Great or Julius Caesar into dust and clay. His words gain sardonic resonance as they are followed by the entry of Claudius and the court, accompanying a coffin.

Hamlet deduces that the incomplete ritual ('maimèd rites') signifies the coffin contains a suicide. His guess is confirmed when the Priest vehemently asserts that, but for Claudius' command, the body would be denied proper Christian burial. As Hamlet had recalled in his first soliloquy, the Church viewed suicide as a sin, and people taking their own lives were damned to suffer eternally in hell. But what the Priest's complaint significantly shows is that in Claudius' Denmark the Church must submit to the state; politics overrides religion. The king's word is all-powerful.

Laertes' furious condemnation of the Priest reveals to Hamlet that the funeral is Ophelia's. The actor must decide how to react to that surprise, and to hearing his mother's words. Gertrude, strewing flowers on the coffin in mourning farewell, declares her hope that Ophelia should have been Hamlet's bride. But hearing Hamlet's name provokes Laertes to another hyperbolic outburst:

> Oh treble woe
> Fall ten times treble on that cursèd head   *(lines 213–14)*

He leaps into the grave to embrace Ophelia. Laertes' flamboyant action and exaggerated language provokes Hamlet to display similar bravura: 'This is I, / Hamlet the Dane.' Laertes assaults him, and Claudius orders the attendants to part the two men. The First Quarto (see page 55) suggests that their fight takes place in the grave, but many critics argue that Laertes climbs out to attack Hamlet. In this scene Shakespeare leaves open the widest range of possibilities for dramatic interpretation: how do Claudius and Gertrude react to Hamlet's sudden appearance? How do they respond to Hamlet's claim to be king of Denmark ('the Dane')? What happens to the Gravedigger?

Shakespeare also leaves much room for speculation about why Hamlet behaves as he does. He was surely shocked to discover the corpse is Ophelia, but do his feelings for her motivate what he says and does? Hamlet matches Laertes' bombast as he declares that his love for Ophelia was infinitely greater than that of 'forty thousand brothers'. He claims he can match any action to prove his love, however improbable: 'Woo't drink up eisel [vinegar], eat a crocodile?'

Gertrude, like Claudius, attributes Hamlet's behaviour to madness, an explanation they both know is false. But Hamlet provides some justification for it in his final enigmatic remark 'The cat will mew, and dog will have his day.' Claudius takes control, secretly assuring Laertes that their murderous plot against Hamlet will shortly be enacted, and publicly instructing Gertrude to set guards on Hamlet, whom he describes as 'your son', not 'our son' as in Act 1. His promise may be both a declaration of an enduring memorial to Ophelia, and a veiled threat against Hamlet's life:

> This grave shall have a living monument.   *(line 264)*

Act 5 Scene 2

The scene begins with Hamlet telling the story of his time at sea to Horatio. Unable to sleep on the ship, he searched Rosencrantz and Guildenstern's cabin for the letter from Claudius. It ordered he should be executed immediately on arrival in England. He wrote another letter, sealing it with his father's royal signet ring, commanding the execution of Rosencrantz and Guildenstern. He placed the substitute letter back in his schoolfellows' cabin, and the next day, in the sea fight, was captured by the pirates.

Such a bare summary conceals important features of Hamlet's conversation with Horatio (in which Horatio seems little more than a 'feed' as he briefly agrees, exclaims or asks questions). Hamlet claims that the will of God, a kind of Christian fate, determines the direction of people's lives. An individual has very little power over what he or she will become:

> There's a divinity that shapes our ends,
> Rough-hew them how we will   *(lines 10–11)*

How far that assertion applies to Hamlet's own situation is questionable. Bradley, for example, seems to argue that Hamlet's personality is the major factor in explaining the course of events. In contrast, accident (the chance meeting with the pirate ship, the possession of the signet ring), not the will of any character, seems to shape the development of the tragedy. Whether these represent the workings of a divine providence, as Hamlet seems to believe, is very much open to debate.

The story also shows Hamlet's characteristic trait of general-ising from a particular incident, however seemingly trivial. His imagery of being trapped in a stage drama ('prologue', 'play') and his explanation of his attitude to legible handwriting might seem undramatic, even though they are revealing of character. A more significant aspect of Hamlet's character is his chilling lack of remorse, or any sense of moral responsibility for the deaths of Rosencrantz and Guildenstern (who may have had no knowledge of what was in Claudius' letter). He dismisses them as mere instruments of Claudius:

> Why man, they did make love to this employment.
> They are not near my conscience. *(lines 57–8)*

For Hamlet, his two schoolfellows are merely 'baser nature', common people who have stumbled between the deadly duel of 'mighty opposites': Hamlet and Claudius. In that fatal combat, Hamlet claims four justifications for taking revenge. He succinctly combines personal with political reasons. Claudius has by trickery stolen his father, mother, throne, and almost his own life:

> He that hath killed my king, and whored my mother,
> Popped in between th'election and my hopes,
> Thrown out his angle for my proper life *(lines 64–6)*

Many critics interpret Hamlet's conversation with Horatio as showing he is a changed man. They see in his regular verse lines that he is calm and quietly determined, with no more doubts about the morality of revenge ('perfect conscience'). He is confident that providence will shortly provide him with the opportunity to kill Claudius in the brief time available before the king learns the news from England ('The interim's mine'). He clear-sightedly views Laertes as a fellow-revenger, and regrets his behaviour towards him.

Shakespeare now introduces a new character, the affected courtier Osric. Hamlet's mocking of the wealthy Osric can be seen as both a condemnation of the corruption at Claudius' court, and also as Shakespeare's barbed criticism of the courtiers of his own time (see page 67). Hamlet's images portray Osric as a flickering lightweight ('water-fly'), gaudy and noisy (a 'chough' is a jackdaw), typical of the flock ('bevy') of frothy and superficial people ('yesty collection') fashionable in these frivolous ('drossy') times. It is a matter for speculation whether the Elizabethan courtiers who attended performances at the Globe recognised themselves in Shakespeare's satirical parody of their pretentious speech and behaviour. What is certain is that many of them had used flattery and corruption to feather their own nests.

Osric tells of a wager Claudius has made. He praises Laertes in such exaggerated courtly language that Hamlet makes fun of him by responding in a style even more elaborate and obscure. Osric seems baffled, but then tells of Claudius' wager: in a twelve-bout duel between Hamlet and Laertes, Laertes will not win three more bouts than Hamlet. Claudius' plot against Hamlet's life is being put into practice, but whether Osric is an innocent messenger, or knows of the murderous trap being set is not clear. Each production makes its own choice.

The unnamed lord who asks if Hamlet is ready to fence, seems, in his plain-spoken courtesy, a deliberate contrast to Osric. Hamlet declares he is ready, but tells Horatio of his uneasiness – does he suspect Claudius' plot? Horatio cautions him to follow his feelings, and offers to give his apologies. But Hamlet, in dignified and simple prose, declares the time is ripe, and accepts whatever fate may have in store for him:

> Not a whit, we defy augury. There is special providence in the fall of a sparrow. If it be now, 'tis not to come; if it be not to come, it will be now; if it be not now, yet it will come – the readiness is all … Let be. *(lines 192–6)*

Critics are divided on whether to see this serenity in the face of death as a stoical fatalism or an acceptance of Christian providence. Whatever the nature of his belief, Hamlet has left the anxieties of the first four acts behind him, and faces the dangerous future with a new-found equanimity.

The entry of the court is usually staged with great ceremony, because Claudius intends to have Hamlet's 'accidental' death take place in the public ritual of a fencing match, witnessed by as many people as possible. Hamlet, obeying his mother's request, asks Laertes to pardon him. He claims his madness, rather than himself, was to blame for the wrongs done to Laertes. Laertes, with reservations, accepts Hamlet's apology.

Both men conceal more than they reveal. Laertes speaks of 'honour', but plans to kill Hamlet by deceit. Hamlet seems to absolve himself of any responsibility for the deaths of Polonius and Ophelia, and his behaviour in the graveyard. He may not have intended harm ('purposed evil'), but much more than his madness was surely to blame. Shakespeare puts the sincerity of each noble revenger into question as they prepare to fight.

The two men choose rapiers. Laertes selects the unblunted blade. Hamlet, as Claudius predicted, does not inspect the weapons closely. As they prepare (and perhaps to give Laertes the opportunity to poison his sword-tip) the king orders wine and noisy celebrations if Hamlet is successful. What Claudius proposes establishes yet again the social context of the play as it recalls Danish history. The boastful ritual of the cannons' challenge to heaven itself is also a reminder that the original Globe audiences expected and enjoyed a noisy display of drums, trumpets and the firing of cannon.

The fencing match and its bloody outcome occupy around only 60 lines, but every production seizes the many opportunities to create thrilling stage action. Here, reactions are as important as actions, and every character, named and unnamed, must work out how they will respond to what they see and hear. The fencing (which sometimes includes comic 'business') can last for several minutes before Hamlet makes the first hit. Claudius can then hold up the action as with great pomp he places the poisoned pearl in the cup, drinks to Hamlet and signals for the drums and trumpets to sound and the cannon to be fired.

There are further opportunities for imaginative stage interpretations as Hamlet declines to drink (is he suspicious?), engages Laertes, and makes another hit. Gertrude's wiping the sweat from her son's face is often staged as a tender moment of mother–son reconciliation. In rehearsal the two actors often spend much time discussing just what impression they wish to convey to the audience in these few lines.

Similarly, the episode in which Gertrude drinks from the poisoned cup, defying Claudius' attempt to stop her, offers another choice. Does she realise the cup is poisoned? Is she deliberately taking her own life? The text gives no indication, but the decision to show her suspicious of her husband can be made theatrically convincing, especially if previous scenes have shown Gertrude progressively distancing herself from Claudius. He is given only the melodramatic aside 'It is too late.' His lack of action suggests that he is more concerned for his own life than his wife's.

Most modern productions show Laertes wounding Hamlet deceitfully, at an interval in the fencing match. In a scuffle, they exchange rapiers. Shakespeare provides no indication that Hamlet realises Laertes' sword-tip is dangerously unprotected ('unbated'), but many productions make that discovery an electrifyingly theatrical moment. Hamlet's wounding of Laertes is often a savagely realistic affair. Sometimes the queen, as she dies, realising the poison was meant for Hamlet, points to Claudius in silent accusation.

Laertes reveals the treacherous plot ('the king, the king's to blame') and Hamlet, often very spectacularly, wounds Claudius. The general shout of 'Treason, treason' provides many opportunities for stage business showing how the court reacts to the sight of the killing of the king. Hamlet has taken his revenge, but it has come about in an unexpected way, and Hamlet himself is mortally wounded.

With his dying words Laertes forgives Hamlet and renounces his role as revenger. Hamlet's three-word farewell to his mother ('Wretched queen adieu') is often made a poignant moment of stage action. He prevents Horatio from committing suicide and, concerned that his reputation should not be tarnished ('wounded name'), asks Horatio to report his story. At the point of death, he declares his support for Fortinbras as king of Denmark:

> But I do prophesy th'election lights
> On Fortinbras; he has my dying voice.   *(lines 334–5)*

That final action held special appeal for Elizabethan audiences, who were greatly concerned with the issue of who should succeed their own ailing monarch. Only two or three years after *Hamlet* was written, Queen Elizabeth, on her deathbed, nominated James I as her successor. But because many productions omit Fortinbras (see pages 92, 100), the lines are often cut, and the performance ends, as it often did in the nineteenth century, with Hamlet's enigmatic final words and Horatio's farewell:

HAMLET   The rest is silence.
HORATIO Now cracks a noble heart. Goodnight sweet prince,
      And flights of angels sing thee to thy rest. –   *(lines 337–9)*

This ending can sometimes seem romantically sentimental. It ignores Shakespeare's emphasis on the political setting of the play, with Fortinbras taking over the state of Denmark. The acknowledgement that the personal tragedy of Hamlet is set in a wider world is signalled by Horatio's next line: 'Why does the drum come hither?' The question is typical of Shakespeare's dramatic construction. It brings a social and military world into immediate conjunction with the religious and very personal mood of the preceding lines. The final 40 lines of the play confirm how utterly interlocked are its private and public dimensions.

The English ambassadors' report that Rosencrantz and Guildenstern are dead reveals how brief an interim Hamlet had to achieve revenge. Horatio's summary of the story he intends to tell promises an account of how individual deaths resulted from personal and political causes. His request to tell it immediately reveals the precarious stability of the Danish state ('men's minds are wild'). Fortinbras' claim to the throne of Denmark can be staged as forecasting either a benign or tyrannical rule ahead. In one production his instruction 'Go bid the soldiers shoot' was an order for Horatio to be taken off and executed. Fortinbras' final praise deepens Hamlet's 'mystery': what was he really like? The play has shown little of his military or royal qualities:

                    Let four captains
      Bear Hamlet like a soldier to the stage,
      For he was likely, had he been put on,
      To have proved most royal   *(lines 374–7)*

Act 5: Critical review

The graveyard scene mixes comedy with tragedy, and is thematically and contextually significant. The physical presence of bones and skulls, and the exchanges between Hamlet and the Gravedigger intensify the play's preoccupation with death and corruption. There is, in the Gravedigger's complaint about 'pocky corses', a reminder that sexually transmitted diseases were rife in Elizabethan England.

The macabre humour acquires a subversive edge as it presents a commoner and a prince talking on equal terms, with the low-status character mocking his superior. The Gravedigger's derisive replies give Hamlet a taste of his own medicine. Shakespeare may be using low-status characters to mock the play itself, stopping it from taking itself too seriously or providing an alternative, ironic viewpoint.

Hamlet's tale of how he returned to Denmark has fascinating implications for explanations of the tragedy. It suggests that the outcome of the play depends on fortune and chance (being captured by pirates) rather than the will of God or any character. It also chillingly conveys Hamlet's casual dismissal of any responsibility for the deaths of Rosencrantz and Guildenstern. His conversation with Horatio also reveals the emotional distance Hamlet has travelled from the troubled mind that asked 'To be or not to be?' to the simple acceptance: 'Let be.' He faces the prospect of death with stoical calm.

On the surface, the final scene of the fencing match and the multiple deaths seems to resolve key issues of the play. Hamlet achieves his revenge, conflict ceases, Claudius' falseness is exposed, and a new ruler, Fortinbras, supported by Hamlet's dying voice, takes over in Denmark. The tragedy seems harmoniously concluded. But Shakespeare's stagecraft prevents such a neat or optimistic ending.

The play acknowledges its own essentially dramatic nature as it leaves interpretation open to theatrical performance. The play's openness to interpretation is encapsulated in Hamlet's final line. It offers a host of potential meanings and moods. It can be spoken to create a sense of romantic heroism or dejected failure, triumphant achievement or tragic waste, calm acceptance or bleak nihilism:

the rest is silence. *(line 337)*

The hugely enjoyable film *Shakespeare in Love* portrays a popular belief about the source of Shakespeare's creativity. It shows him suffering from 'writer's block', unable to put pen to paper, with no idea of how to write his next play. But all is resolved when he meets a beautiful young girl. His love for her sparks an overwhelming flow of creative energy – and he writes *Romeo and Juliet*!

It is an attractive idea, and the film presents it delightfully, but the truth of the matter is far more complex. Like every other writer, Shakespeare was influenced by many factors other than his own personal experience. The society of his time, its practices, beliefs and language in political and economic affairs, culture and religion, were the raw materials on which his imagination worked.

This section first identifies the three texts from which all later editions of *Hamlet* derive. It then discusses the contexts from which *Hamlet* emerged: the wide range of different influences which fostered the creativity of Shakespeare as he wrote the play.

What did Shakespeare write?

Sometime around 1600, William Shakespeare, already a successful playwright, wrote *Hamlet*. It was probably first performed in 1601 on the stage of the Globe Theatre on London's Bankside. What was the play that Shakespeare wrote and his Globe audiences heard? No one knows for certain because his original script has not survived, nor have any handwritten amendments he might subsequently have made. What exists are three published versions of the play, known as the First Quarto, the Second Quarto and the First Folio (a quarto page is about the same size as this page you are reading, a folio page is around two times larger). All later published editions of the play use these texts, particularly the Second Quarto and First Folio, to present their own version of *Hamlet*.

The First Quarto is often known as the 'bad quarto'. Published in 1603, it is often thought to be a 'pirate' version, compiled by two actors (one of whom probably played Marcellus) who wanted to cash in on the play's success on stage and so tried to reconstruct it from memory. It is short (under 2,200 lines), some characters' names are unfamiliar, and well-known speeches look very different. For example, its version of Hamlet's best-known soliloquy begins:

> To be, or not to be, I there's the point,
> To die, to sleep, is that all? I all:
> No, to sleepe, to dreame, I marry there it goes ...

Generally, editors make very limited use of the First Quarto, often describing it as garbled and corrupt. But it is often thought valuable for the clues it contains on how the play was staged. These clues include the stage directions for Ophelia's entry in her first mad scene: 'playing on a lute, and her hair down singing'; for the Ghost's appearance in the closet scene: 'Enter the ghost in his night-gown'; and for Hamlet's behaviour in the graveyard: 'leaps in after Laertes to Ophelia's grave'. The other versions do not contain any such clues.

The Second Quarto of 1604 is usually thought to be Shakespeare's company's response to the 'bad quarto'. Many scholars regard it as a kind of 'official' version, based on Shakespeare's original manuscript or a copy of it, and intended to establish the authentic version of the play. It claims to be printed 'according to the true and perfect copy', and contains just under 3,700 lines.

The First Folio was published in 1623, seven years after Shakespeare's death. The volume contains 36 plays, and its version of *Hamlet* is thought to be the result of Shakespeare's own revisions in the light of performance experience. It is shorter than the Second Quarto by around 220 lines. Speeches that do not appear include Hamlet's soliloquy after seeing Fortinbras' army: 'How all occasions do inform against me' (Act 4 Scene 4), and his reflections on 'some vicious mole of nature' in the battlements scene (Act 1 Scene 4). But the First Folio includes 83 lines not in the Second Quarto (including 'Denmark's a prison' and the 'little eyases' episode).

So the text of *Hamlet* is not as stable as you might think. Indeed, there is no such thing as *the* text, but rather, there are several *texts*. Whatever edition of the play you are using, it will vary from what Shakespeare actually wrote and from other editions. This is no reason for dismay, but rather an opportunity to think about how this uncertainty reflects the play itself. In the same way that Hamlet searches for truth, but discovers different possible meanings, so the text has always been presented on the page in different ways. Performances of the play even more closely mirror that openness to variety of presentation. Every production is different as each selects, cuts and amends to present its own unique version of *Hamlet*.

Today, many scholars argue against 'conflation' (the practice of combining Quarto and Folio versions), claiming that the First Folio is Shakespeare's final acting version. But virtually all stage and film productions and most printed editions do in fact 'conflate' in some way. What is helpful for study is a version that presents, as clearly but unobtrusively as possible, the Second Quarto and Folio versions. For that reason this Guide follows the New Cambridge edition of the play (also used in Cambridge School Shakespeare) which is based on the Folio, and includes, in square brackets, lines found only in the Second Quarto.

What did Shakespeare read?

Shakespeare's genius lay in his ability to transform what he read into gripping drama. This section is therefore about the influence of genre: the literary and dramatic contexts of *Hamlet*. It identifies the story, plays and dramatic conventions that fired Shakespeare's imagination as he wrote *Hamlet*.

A story of revenge: Saxo Grammaticus

Hamlet is based on a twelfth-century revenge story about an early Prince of Denmark, Amleth. The tale, by Saxo Grammaticus, was published in Latin in 1514, but most scholars believe that Shakespeare read a 1570 French version of the story by François de Belleforest. The old story has very recognisable similarities with Hamlet:

Amleth's father is King of Denmark. He defeats the King of Norway in a duel, but is murdered by Feng, his own brother. Feng quickly marries the queen, Gerutha, Amleth's mother. In pursuit of revenge, Amleth feigns madness (in Danish, Amleth meant 'simpleton' or idiot). But his language is such a mixture of insanity and cleverness that he is tested in various ways.

In the first test, a 'fair woman' is sent to him, with the purpose of finding out if he will behave normally to her. He reveals to her that he is really sane, but he makes her swear she will not reveal his secret. Next, one of Feng's friends hides in Amleth's mother's bedroom in order to overhear Amleth's private conversation with his mother. Amleth pretends to be a cockerel, finds the spy under a straw mattress, kills him, chops him up, cooks him and feeds him to the pigs piece by piece.

Amleth strongly condemns his mother for not being faithful to her first husband's memory and for so swiftly marrying Feng after being widowed. Feng becomes even more suspicious of Amleth and plots to kill him by sending him to England with two servants. The servants bear a secret instruction from Feng to the King of England, ordering Amleth's immediate death. Amleth steals the messengers' document and rewrites it, ordering their deaths. He also adds a request that the daughter of the English king should marry Amleth.

Eventually Amleth returns to Denmark – to discover his own funeral is taking place! He battles successfully with members of Feng's court, destroys the palace by fire, seeks out Feng, whom he finds in bed, and kills him, so achieving revenge. Afterwards Amleth hides, uncertain of how the people of Denmark will view his deeds. At last he comes out of hiding and makes a public speech to defend and justify what he has done. The people are delighted, feeling that Amleth has freed them from Feng's tyranny. They declare Amleth king. He has a long and successful reign, ending only when he is killed in battle.

Shakespeare made many changes to turn the story into tragic drama, most notably:

- inventing the Ghost, who orders Hamlet to revenge;
- adding young Fortinbras and Laertes: both revengers;
- adding the Players and the play-within-a-play;
- making Ophelia a major character;
- adding a comic Gravedigger who prompts Hamlet's broodings on mortality;
- having Hamlet mortally wounded only moments before he achieves his revenge;
- setting the play in Christian times when personal revenge and suicide are forbidden.

Shakespeare's additions need to be understood in the context of the Elizabethan appetite for revenge tragedy. Audiences flocked to such plays; it was a hugely popular genre. Shakespeare had already written one bloodsoaked revenge tragedy in the early 1590s: *Titus Andronicus*. The popular demand that existed for tragedies provides a general reason why Shakespeare wrote *Hamlet*. But it is possible to identify several particular theatrical influences on the play. They are the tragedies of the Roman dramatist, Seneca; Thomas Kyd's hugely popular play *The Spanish Tragedy*; and a play, now lost, which is known as the *Ur-Hamlet*.

Revenge tragedies: Seneca (4 BC–AD 65)

A collection of Seneca's tragedies was published in 1581, and the plays increasingly enjoyed popular success on stage. Seneca found the material for his tragic dramas in Greek mythology, but his reworking of those ancient tales was done in a startling manner which greatly appealed to Elizabethan audiences. Seneca's impact on English playwrights, including Shakespeare, was profound, and many revenge plays imitated his example. All the following features of Senecan drama can be detected in some form in *Hamlet*:

- a ghost appears calling for revenge
- revenge dominates characters' motives, and provides dramatic suspense
- revengers use exaggerated and hyperbolic language
- characters descend into madness
- the use of a play-within-a-play
- displays of violence that resulted in a corpse-strewn stage
- a five-part structure, approximately as follows:
  - Act 1 a ghost appeals for vengeance
  - Act 2 the revenger plans revenge
  - Act 3 the confrontation of avenger and victim
  - Act 4 vengeance is prevented
  - Act 5 revenge is completed

The Spanish Tragedy: Thomas Kyd (1558–94)

Of all the plays inspired by Seneca, by far the most successful in the early 1590s was Thomas Kyd's *The Spanish Tragedy*. It was a theatrical sensation, a bloodthirsty cliffhanger which was also a searching examination of the relationship between revenge and justice. The main character, Hieronimo, the Knight Marshal of Spain, is driven into madness by the murder of his son Horatio. Hieronimo cannot obtain justice from the gods or the king, and so determines to achieve personal revenge. He prepares a play in which he will wreak vengeance on his son's killers:

> Behoves thee then, Hieronomo, to be revenged.
> The plot is laid of dire revenge:
> On then, Hieronimo, pursue revenge,
> For nothing wants but acting of revenge.

Like Seneca's plays, *The Spanish Tragedy* contains a ghost calling for revenge, a play-within-a-play, madness and bloodshed. There are all kinds of gruesome events: hangings, suicides, a near burning at the stake, multiple stabbings. The play focuses relentlessly on the working out of revenge. Revenge appears as a character, as a kind of Chorus and director of the action. Almost everyone in the play seeks revenge, prompted by all kinds of different motives: honour, love, envy, anger and grief. The language is Senecan: exaggerated, hyperbolic, rhetorical.

The Spanish Tragedy demonstrates how much audiences enjoyed plays in which murder breeds murder and almost every character intends harm to others. Its astonishing success undoubtedly influenced Shakespeare, and in *Hamlet* he took over but transformed many of the elements of Kyd's tragic model. Perhaps the most obvious transformation is in having a son (Hamlet) seeking revenge for his murdered father, rather than having a father (Hieronimo) seeking revenge for his murdered son as in Kyd's play. Kyd's bloodcurdler has virtually vanished from the theatre, but its influence on Hamlet is hinted at in the following key features:

- the close linking of justice and revenge
- the presentation of revenge as a sacred duty, where an individual, denied justice, takes the law into his own hands
- the portrayal of a hesitant revenger
- madness
- extremes of emotion
- deceit and intrigue
- a play-within-a-play to further the revenge plot
- the supernatural

A lost play: the *Ur-Hamlet*

A play of *Hamlet* existed at least ten years before Shakespeare's play. It is known as the *Ur-Hamlet* (*Ur* means 'early'). Evidence for its existence comes from several sources. In 1589 Thomas Nash dismissively criticised the English dramatists who were writing Seneca-like plays and who 'will afford you whole Hamlets, I should say handfuls, of tragical speeches'. In 1596 Thomas Lodge commented on a character who

> walks for the most part in black under the cover of gravity, and looks as pale as the vizard of the ghost who cried so miserably at the Theatre like an oyster-wife, 'Hamlet, revenge!'

The *Ur-Hamlet* may have been written by Thomas Kyd or some other dramatist, or even by Shakespeare himself. No one knows. Shakespeare may have reworked this old play, or at least may have had it in his mind as he wrote *Hamlet*. But with the creation of *Hamlet*, Shakespeare moved tragedy far beyond the blood-boltered melodramas of the early 1590s. In his scepticism and moral self-questioning, in his doubt about the truthfulness of a ghost, and uncertainty about whether to obey the command to revenge, Hamlet is radically different from Elizabethan drama's earlier revengers.

What was Shakespeare's England like?

Shakespeare's own audiences, watching performances at the Globe in 1601, would recognise certain aspects of their own world which they took for granted. Like Laertes asking for Claudius' 'leave and favour to return to France', an English citizen similarly had to ask for permission to travel abroad. When Hamlet reminds Osric to put his hat on, Elizabethans would see not only mockery, but a reminder of a social rule: a gentleman kept his hat on in another gentleman's presence, but removed it when meeting royalty. In the play's references to 'fortune', audiences would be reminded of the many drawings and emblems portraying the goddess of chance and the wheel of fortune: familiar iconography.

Similarly, listening to Hamlet's question to the Gravedigger, 'How long will a man lie i'th'earth ere he rot?', and watching him contemplating the skull of Yorick, Elizabethan audiences would not think Hamlet uniquely morbid. Such questions and behaviour were commonplace. Shakespeare's contemporaries were preoccupied with death and decay in ways that in western society today are unfamiliar and often abhorrent. They looked human mortality squarely in the face. Disease and death were ever-present for most families. The average life expectancy was little more than 30 years, there was a high infant death rate, and the plague was a regular visitor to city and country alike. With death such a familiar experience, skeletons and skulls frequently figured in paintings and woodcuts, and tomb sculptures often portrayed the physical signs of human decay. People kept, or gave each other, a memento mori: a reminder of mortality, such as a small, carved death's head.

Elizabethans would recognise the scraps of popular songs and ballads in the play. Hamlet's philosophising reflected Elizabethans' endless curiosity about the idea of the 'self', and about a character type: 'the melancholy man'. But there are deeper ways than such reminders of everyday life in which *Hamlet* reveals what Elizabethan England was like, and how it helped shape the play. Hamlet describes the players as 'the abstract and brief chronicles of the time': they show, in dramatic form, the nature of Elizabethan society. Later, in his advice to the actors, he defines 'the purpose of playing':

> to hold as 'twere the mirror up to nature; to show virtue her
> own feature, scorn her own image, and the very age and body
> of the time his form and pressure.   *(Act 3 Scene 2, lines 18–20)*

Hamlet's definition works for both the fictional world of the play and for the condition of Elizabethan England. The play-within-a-play discloses what Claudius' Elsinore is like, but it also gives insight into the 'form and pressure' of Shakespeare's own times: the social, intellectual and cultural contexts that influenced the creation of *Hamlet*.

Hamlet's Denmark can be compared to Shakespeare's England. Both were transitional societies, caught up in a fundamental process of change. In Denmark, old King Hamlet had ruled over a feudal, chivalrous world in which disputes were settled by personal combat. In Claudius' new world, conflict was to be resolved by diplomacy and scheming. Shakespeare's England was similarly an emerging modern world in which medieval certainties were yielding to scepticism and doubt.

Hamlet's own preoccupation with sin and salvation shows he is the product of a feudal world where religion was used as an instrument of control. But his style of thought, full of doubt and scepticism, marks him out as a self-conscious modern individual. He continually debates with himself, questioning what he sees, hears and thinks. In a series of soliloquies he opens his thoughts and feelings to searching examination by himself and by the audience. That introspection and constant uncertainty about beliefs which he had previously taken for granted mark him out as a 'modern' man. In Elizabethan England, both individuals and society were changing radically from their medieval origins.

That process of change was accelerated by the discoveries of science and exploration. The observations and experiments of such scientists as Copernicus and Galileo had disproved medieval belief that human beings were at the centre of a fixed and stable cosmos. The voyages of Columbus and later navigators had discovered new worlds and cultures, further shaking the firm convictions of the medieval world.

This unsettling of old, confidently-held beliefs was further fostered by developments in art, philosophy and learning inspired by the rediscovery of the classical world of Greece and Rome. The traditional way of describing the cultural changes which took place between the fourteenth and the sixteenth century has been to speak of the Renaissance ('rebirth'). That description has been applied to Shakespeare's England, and Hamlet is often interpreted as a typical Renaissance man, trapped between celebrating the glories of earth and humanity, and anguishing over doubts and uncertainties:

> this most excellent canopy the air, look you, this
> brave o'erhanging firmament, this majestical roof fretted with
> golden fire – why, it appeareth no other thing to me but a foul
> and pestilent congregation of vapours. What a piece of work is
> a man! How noble in reason, how infinite in faculties, in form
> and moving how express and admirable, in action how like an
> angel, in apprehension how like a god! The beauty of the

world, the paragon of animals – and yet to me, what is this
quintessence of dust? Man delights not me …

(Act 2 Scene 2, lines 283–91)

Today, many scholars increasingly prefer to describe Shakespeare's
own times as the 'early modern period' (not as Renaissance England),
and to see Hamlet as an early modern man. 'Early modern'
acknowledges that Shakespeare's England contains the seeds of the
modern world, whereas 'Renaissance' implies the restoration of the
older, classical world. The choice of description is claimed to be a
significant, not a trivial matter, and is justified in two ways:

- 'Renaissance' implies looking backward to earlier ages, whereas
  Elizabethan England was very obviously showing signs of
  modernity: complexity, scepticism and doubt. Hamlet, like early
  modern England, displays misgivings about the ethics of revenge,
  the nature of ghosts, the justification of divine and secular
  authority, and the stability of social order.
- 'Early modern' takes account of the economic developments of the
  time. These include the growth of early capitalism, the opening up
  of new markets by the voyages of exploration, and the subsequent
  colonisation and exploitation of the Americas and Africa. In
  contrast, 'Renaissance' tends to be associated only with aesthetic
  and artistic matters.

Politics and the court

Watching *Hamlet*, Elizabethan audiences would feel many resonances
with their own world. England, like Denmark, was a troubled country.
As the play opens, Denmark fears a foreign invasion. In England,
although the Spanish Armada had been defeated in 1588, alarms still
persisted about a renewed invasion attempt.

Threats of war from abroad were compounded by threats from
within. Although seemingly stable, Claudius' Denmark, like
Elizabethan England, is dangerously insecure. Only moments after
Claudius has spoken of sorrows coming 'not single spies, but in
battalions' a 'rabble' of ordinary citizens break in, demanding that
Laertes become king. England, towards the end of Queen Elizabeth's
reign, had even more powerful battalions of sorrows that threatened
internal stability. There was constant anxiety about the problem of

succession: just who should rule England when the old monarch died? Whoever succeeded would inherit a dangerously discontented country.

The threats came from groups at all levels of England's sharply hierarchical social structure. Active protest, hazardous to the stability of the state, came from the rich and powerful few, and the poor and dispossessed many. Around the time *Hamlet* was first performed, the Earl of Essex led an abortive rebellion against Elizabeth. As a prologue to the attempted coup, the rebels paid Shakespeare's company to perform *Richard II*, with its scene of the deposition of a king. Some critics speculate that Hamlet is a reflection of Essex's inner life and his reputation for refusing to make up his mind (but such a claim cannot be proved).

At the other end of the social scale, riots and crime were provoked by poverty, enclosures of common land, recurring harvest failures, food shortages and unemployment. Profound religious differences added further possibilities for conflict. Social reality was very different from the myth of Merrie England ruled over by Good Queen Bess.

Hamlet mirrors the anxieties of Shakespeare's England. Claudius' murder of Old Hamlet was a political assassination to achieve political power. The watching audience would have heard of numerous assassination plots laid against the life of Elizabeth. In a society with no television or newspapers, news passed mainly by word of mouth, and gossip and rumours flourished. Many false stories about Queen Elizabeth's ill-health spread like wildfire. Claudius' description of the angry Laertes, all too ready to listen to rumour-mongers ('buzzers'), was highly recognisable to an Elizabethan audience as a picture of a discontented nobleman like the Earl of Essex:

> Feeds on his wonder, keeps himself in clouds,
> And wants not buzzers to infect his ear
>
> *(Act 4 Scene 5, lines 88–9)*

In this atmosphere of suspicion, and fear of insurrection, it was not surprising that the state wished to control news and debate. Free discussion was seen by those in power as a potential source of treason. Fictional Denmark mirrored Elizabethan England in its efforts to detect and defeat subversion. In both societies, the right-hand man of the monarch believed that order was maintained by close surveillance. Polonius is often compared to Lord Burghley, Elizabeth's chief minister of state.

Just as Burghley maintained an extensive network of spies and informers, so Polonius is infected by the same desire to overhear in secret, to keep all potential dissidents under surveillance. He secretly spies on Hamlet, using his own daughter Ophelia as bait. And just as Burghley had written moral precepts for his son, and set spies to report on his behaviour in France, so Polonius lectures Laertes and sends Reynaldo to spy on him in Paris. His boastful description of himself and the roundabout ways and indirect methods he uses to discover the truth reflect the procedures of the actual spymaster of the Tudor state:

> And thus do we of wisdom and of reach,
> With windlasses and with assays of bias,
> By indirections find directions out.   *(Act 2 Scene 1, lines 62–7)*

That description of the devious methods used by the state to maintain control would carry echoes of Machiavellianism for an Elizabethan audience. Niccolò Machiavelli's *The Prince* (1532) was a handbook for rulers about the use of deceit in statecraft. Machiavelli urged rulers to use any means, however unethical or immoral, to stay in power. His instruction in practical politics was a set of ruthless and manipulative prescriptions to ensure no one could succeed in overthrowing a monarch.

Even to those who had not read Machiavelli's book, its purpose and argument were well known. In the drama of Elizabethan England, the machiavel (a villainous plotter and schemer) became a familiar figure who delighted in wrongdoing and used poison, sword or torture to achieve his ends. Portrayals of scheming and unscrupulous foreigners greatly appealed to the English audiences of the time, and were an expected part of drama. Shakespeare achieved new levels of subtlety and complexity in his presentation of the plotting and counterplotting of Hamlet and Claudius. Audiences would recognise the Machiavellian quality of the king's subtle corruption of Laertes, and his plot to use a duel to kill Hamlet with an unbated sword and poisoned cup and yet avoid blame:

> I will work him
> To an exploit, now ripe in my device,
> Under the which he shall not choose but fall,
> And for his death no wind of blame shall breathe,
> But even his mother shall uncharge the practice
> And call it accident.
> *(Act 4 Scene 7, lines 62–7)*

The critic Dover Wilson argues that an Elizabethan audience would have seen the entry of the Danish court in Act 1 Scene 2 as like a meeting of Queen Elizabeth and her Privy Council. They would therefore think of the constitution of Denmark as like that of England, and so see that 'Hamlet was the rightful heir to the throne and Claudius a usurper'. But for much of the play Hamlet seems to have little interest in the question of succession. It is not until the final scene that he expresses resentment, and even then, his comment ('Popped in between th'election and my hopes') reveals that Denmark is an elective monarchy in which the king is chosen by the voices of an elite. Unlike England's hereditary monarchy, the throne was not automatically Hamlet's by right of birth.

The correspondence between Elizabethan England and Shakespeare's Denmark is not, of course, exact. But courts then, as now, held a fascination for the populace. There was intense interest in doings of the monarch and the court. The London audiences gossiped about it and enjoyed court scandals. Watching plays about kings and queens fed that desire, and in *Hamlet* they saw other echoes of the court. What is open to interpretation is whether their attitude, or Shakespeare's, was ironic and subversive, critical of the court of Elizabeth.

Osric may well be a mocking portrayal of the sycophancy (servile and fawning flattery) of corrupt and scheming courtiers who used their position at court to improve their social standing and wealth. Distrust and suspicion were widespread as courtiers competed with each other for Queen Elizabeth's favour. She kept some measure of financial and moral control over the worst extravagances of her nobles, but even in her time the reputation of the court for rottenness was widespread. In 1592 Thomas Nashe, in *Pierce Pennilesse his Supplication to the Devil*, said that a courtier's companions were 'Pride, Riot and Whoredom'.

The court was the centre of aristocratic display and conspicuous consumption. Courtiers revelled in extravagant luxury, flaunting their wealth in extravagant, costly dress. Machiavelli had claimed that political power was maintained through display and spectacle. Queen Elizabeth's court confirmed that claim. Music, dancing, plays and masques (spectacular and costly entertainments) were a prime feature of Elizabeth's court. The appeal of such displays is reflected in the dumb show (which is a kind of masque) and the play-within-a-play. Some critics argue that the play can be interpreted as criticism of such extravagance, showing that outward appearance does not match inner reality. Hamlet knows he has 'that within which passes show', and dismisses clothes as 'trappings'.

Revenge

Hamlet is a tragedy, and it is about revenge, but it does not fit neatly into the category of revenge tragedy. Unlike conventional revengers, Hamlet does not obsessively pursue vengeance. He delays, beset by all kinds of doubts and distractions. An Elizabethan audience would be alert to Hamlet's perplexity over the command to revenge, because Hamlet's Denmark resembled Elizabethan England in its point of view on revenge. Personal revenge was forbidden both by the state and the Church, which held that either the law or God would punish wrongdoers. In addition, the Church defined revenge as a sin, and damned revengers to suffer for all eternity. So Hamlet, seeking revenge for his murdered father, was trapped in a dilemma. There could be no justice from the state, because the murderer himself was now king. To take personal revenge meant eternal damnation.

For the Elizabethans, the fact that the command to revenge was delivered by a ghost, added suspicion. They knew that it was in the tradition of revenge tragedy that ghosts called for revenge, but they also possessed a great distrust of ghosts. Many believed that ghosts simply did not exist. Others believed that ghosts were the agents of the Devil, sent to trap men into doing evil.

Revenge also had contemporary echoes for Elizabethans. As they heard the Ghost tell his story, many in the audience would recall the similarities with King James of Scotland (who became king of England in 1603). His own father had been murdered, and his mother, the murdered man's wife (Mary, Queen of Scots) had married the murderer. As a ten-year-old child, James, like Hamlet, had also sworn to revenge his father's murder.

Incest

Hamlet possesses distinctly Elizabethan attitudes towards incest. The watching spectators at the Globe in 1601, hearing in the second scene of the play that Gertrude has married her dead husband's brother, would experience a feeling of intense moral revulsion. The marriage of brother-in-law and sister-in-law was forbidden by the Church, and regarded as incest. Sermons in church regularly condemned it as adultery, and offenders were subjected to cruel rituals of public penance, sometimes carted around the town to be mocked, humiliated and assaulted with missiles. Some members of the audience would endorse the Ghost's description of Claudius as 'that incestuous, that adulterous beast'.

One event long ago had made abhorrence of incest an ever-present issue for Elizabethans. In 1533 Henry VIII had used incest as grounds for the annulment of his marriage to Catherine of Aragon, so freeing himself to marry Anne Boleyn (their child was to become Queen Elizabeth). Catherine had been married to Henry's brother, Arthur. When Arthur died, Henry married Catherine. After 24 years of marriage, wanting to marry Anne, Henry appealed to the incest taboo, quoting the biblical verse that condemned a man's marriage to his brother's wife as unclean and divinely cursed. Some audience members, hearing the Ghost speak against the royal bed of Denmark being used for 'damned incest', would recall a similar warning for the royal bed of England.

Shakespeare adds another impropriety to the marriage. For many Elizabethans, the untimely haste with which Gertrude and Claudius had married would be both shocking and scandalous. They had transgressed not only moral and religious prohibitions, but also rules of decorum (acceptable social behaviour). Widows were expected to observe a lengthy period of mourning, and to dress in black. Gertrude and Claudius seem to have had little regard for either convention. Hamlet is properly dressed in black on his first appearance, and his disgust would be understood by all the audience, and probably shared by many as he repeatedly and obsessively condemns both the haste and the nature of the marriage.

Religion

Since Henry VIII's break with Rome in the 1530s, with the exception of the six-year reign of Queen Mary, England had been a Protestant country. Protestantism made individuals responsible for the state of their souls, yet less assured of what lay in store for them after death. The image of Hamlet contemplating the skull ('Alas poor Yorick!') symbolises crucial aspects of human consciousness in Shakespeare's time: the preoccupation with individual identity, and the lack of certainty of what would happen after death. His 'To be or not to be' soliloquy vividly expresses that uncertainty:

> Who would fardels bear,
> To grunt and sweat under a weary life,
> But that the dread of something after death,
> The undiscovered country from whose bourn
> No traveller returns, puzzles the will,
> And makes us rather bear those ills we have
> Than fly to others that we know not of?
> Thus conscience does make cowards of us all
>
> *(Act 3 Scene 1, lines 76–83)*

Crucial aspects of the religious beliefs of Elizabethan England pervade the play. Suicide was condemned by the Church, and suicides were believed to go straight to hell. In his first soliloquy Hamlet shows awareness of the Church's view that God prohibited suicide:

> Or that the Everlasting had not fixed
> His canon 'gainst self-slaughter.   *(Act 1 Scene 2, lines 131–2)*

The consequences of that belief are sharply expressed in the graveyard scene. The Gravediggers' talk reveals that suicides are normally denied the right to 'Christian burial' in a churchyard. Only the king's command and Ophelia's high social status have allowed her to be buried in consecrated ground. But the Priest, convinced that she took her own life, denies her the full rites of Christian burial:

> She should in ground unsanctified have lodged
> Till the last trumpet. For charitable prayers,
> Shards, flints, and pebbles should be thrown on her.
>
> *(Act 5 Scene 1, lines 196–8)*

Although England was officially Protestant, many citizens still adhered to Catholicism, and Shakespeare incorporates the Catholic notion of Purgatory and confession into the play. Persons who had not made full confession of their sins before dying were believed to go to Purgatory, where they suffered until their unconfessed sins were burnt away ('purged'). Hamlet's father, in the form of the Ghost, tells how he had been killed at a moment when he was unprepared for heaven, and as a consequence he suffers torments in Purgatory. When Hamlet finds Claudius at prayer, he refrains from killing him for fear of sending him direct to heaven. Hamlet sheathes his sword and decides to wait, to catch Claudius at a moment that will damn his soul and condemn him to the same torments Hamlet's father suffers:

> When he is drunk asleep, or in his rage,
> Or in th'incestuous pleasure of his bed,
> At game a-swearing, or about some act
> That has no relish of salvation in't –
> Then trip him that his heels may kick at heaven
>
> *(Act 3 Scene 3, lines 89–93)*

But irrespective of whether a person was Protestant or Catholic, virtually everybody in England cared passionately about religious belief. Religion was ever present, a source of both comfort and anxiety. People worried about the state of their souls, about sin, and about what would happen after death. The question of salvation obsessed them: would they go to heaven or hell? Their anxiety was increased by the loss of the certainty that religion once afforded. For Protestants, death was especially terrifying because Protestantism taught the value of the individual conscience, and so heightened the sense of individual uniqueness. For many Protestants, this awareness of personal identity made death a tragedy of extinction, because it destroyed all those qualities that made up and were valued by individuals: the inner qualities of love, self, imagination. Hamlet's soliloquy 'To be or not to be' expresses the fears of those Protestants who had rejected the old certainties, but were still unsure of what would happen after death.

In the play's final act, after all his doubts and hesitations, Hamlet declares his conviction that heaven guides him. He lists the wrongs that Claudius has committed (killed his father, made his mother a whore, denied Hamlet the crown and tried to kill him). He then declares his confidence that he is fully justified in killing the king. He claims that if he does not kill Claudius he will be damned, as heaven itself demands that Claudius be prevented from committing further evil:

> He that hath killed my king, and whored my mother,
> Popped in between th'election and my hopes,
> Thrown out his angle for my proper life,
> And with such cozenage – is't not perfect conscience
> To quit him with this arm? And is't not to be damned
> To let this canker of our nature come
> In further evil?   *(Act 5 Scene 2, lines 64–70)*

The subordination of women

Hamlet reflects the subordinate position of women in Elizabethan England, where husbands and fathers strictly controlled the lives of wives and daughters. Women's status and roles were subject to the tyranny of patriarchy (rule by men). Their rights were restricted, legally, socially and economically. Gertrude and Ophelia have little or no power or autonomy. Like their Elizabethan counterparts, they are subject to the authority of men. Gertrude only disobeys Claudius once, when she chooses to drink from the poisoned cup. Ophelia is lectured by her brother and her father; her duty is to obey (notice how often she uses 'my lord'). Like most Elizabethan women, she is regarded as a man's possession: Polonius speaks as if she were one of his cattle when he plots to use her as a bait to spy on Hamlet: 'I'll loose my daughter to him'. You can find a more extended discussion of the consequences of such gender discrimination on pages 96–9.

Theatre

Hamlet contains much evidence of Shakespeare's interest in the theatre. The arrival of the players and the performance of *The Murder of Gonzago* are crucial to the plot, as Hamlet proposes to 'catch the conscience of the king' with the play. References to playing and acting resound throughout the play in dramatic images and language: 'show', 'perform', 'prologue', 'part' (see pages 77 and 99–100). With its preoccupation with appearance and reality, with pretence and seeming, *Hamlet* echoes the nature of drama itself. For this reason, some critics describe *Hamlet* as 'metatheatre' (theatre about theatre), and focus their attention on what they see as the play's self-consciousness about theatre.

A striking theatrical example occurs in Hamlet's exchange with Rosencrantz and Guildenstern (Act 2 Scene 2, lines 295–333). Hamlet asks why the players are forced to travel, and why their reputation ('estimation') has declined. He is told it is because of 'an eyrie of children, little eyases, that cry out on the top of question' (a nest of child actors, as noisy as unfledged hawks). This was a company of boy players, very active around the time Shakespeare was writing *Hamlet*, who enjoyed great success in London. For a short time these 'little eyases' threatened the livelihood of some adult professional acting companies which were forced to tour because they could not attract London audiences. The same episode is also thought to be about the 'wars of the theatres' in which the rivalry between adult companies led to intense mocking of each other, or 'much throwing about of brains' as Guildenstern describes it.

Language

The language of the play is full of variety. It shifts constantly from one register to another. Sometimes it is ambiguous or enigmatic, at other times plain and direct. It can be formal and ceremonious, as in Claudius' first address to the court or the First Player's speeches. In contrast, it can be conversational, even colloquial, as in Hamlet's dialogue with the Gravedigger or his friendly greeting of Rosencrantz and Guildenstern. Heightened, bombastic language, full of hyperbole ('Now could I drink hot blood') recalls traditional revenge tragedy. Verse mingles with prose. Dialogue and soliloquy contribute to the play's linguistic diversity.

Like the play itself, the language seems to move at different speeds. It can appear to dawdle or to accelerate rapidly. There are violent exclamations, careful thinking through a problem, and apparently leisurely digressions as characters seem to get sidetracked, as for example in Hamlet's reflection on 'some vicious mole of nature' in particular men, or his conversation about the 'little eyases'. But such 'irrelevancies' always prove to be important to the development of character, theme and atmosphere.

The language embodies the changing emotional climate of the play and of the characters. Sorrow, depression, passion, wit and friendship are just a few of the moods the language expresses. Characters are given distinctive manners of speaking. Polonius' repetitiveness and moralising create a character who clearly likes the sound of his own voice, earning Gertrude's rebuke 'More matter with less art'. Those few words add an extra dimension to Gertrude's own character, but it is Hamlet's language that displays by far the greatest range of variation in the play. In a single soliloquy ('O what a rogue and peasant slave am I!') he moves through self-condemnation, amazement, anger, agonised self-accusation, impassioned fury, mocking self-criticism, deep reflection and determination.

Throughout the play Hamlet switches between very different language styles, often mimicking other characters. He listens to himself and others and revels in the slipperiness of language which gives potential for bitter or comic puns or ironic retorts. He uses puns to great effect, picking up a speaker's words and giving them back with a different meaning. His very first words 'A little more than kin, and less than kind' imply that Claudius is too presumptuous in calling him 'son' (kin), and that his nature (kind) is unlike Claudius'. His next line 'I am too much i'th'sun' puns on Claudius' 'son'. His following two replies to Gertrude pun ironically on her use of 'common' and 'seems'. The Gravedigger is the only other character in the play to use this style of 'deliberate misunderstanding', and gives Hamlet a taste of his own medicine.

Ben Jonson famously remarked that Shakespeare 'wanted art' (lacked technical skill). But that comment is mistaken, as is the popular image of Shakespeare as a 'natural' writer, utterly spontaneous, inspired only by his imagination. Shakespeare possessed a deep knowledge of the language techniques of his and previous times. Behind the apparent effortlessness of the language lies a deeply practised skill. What follows are some of the language techniques he uses in *Hamlet* to intensify dramatic effect, relate events, enact deeds and create mood and character.

Imagery

Hamlet abounds in imagery: vivid words and phrases that help create the atmosphere of the play as they conjure up emotionally-charged pictures in the imagination. At the very start of the play, the sentry Francisco replies to the question whether he has had quiet guard:

> Not a mouse stirring.　　　*(Act 1 Scene 1, line 10)*

Francisco's image is the first of the many word pictures that characterise the play. Shakespeare's unflagging and richly varied use of verbal illustration stirs the audience's imagination throughout *Hamlet* and deepens dramatic impact. Sometimes he uses stories: the Ghost's tale of poisoning; Ophelia's depiction of Hamlet's 'mad' appearance and behaviour; Gertrude's lyrical description of Ophelia's drowning. Most often he uses images to enrich emotional force and intensify meaning:

> He would drown the stage with tears　　*(Act 2 Scene 2, line 514)*
> For who would bear the whips and scorns of time
> 　　　　　　　　　　　　　　　*(Act 3 Scene 1, line 70)*
> A king of shreds and patches　　*(Act 3 Scene 4, line 102)*

All Shakespeare's imagery uses metaphor, simile or personification. All are comparisons. A simile compares one thing to another using 'like' or 'as' (the Ghost describes the poison's working: 'swift as quicksilver', 'like eager droppings into milk'). A metaphor is also a comparison, suggesting that two dissimilar things are actually the same ('Denmark's a prison'). Personification turns all kinds of things into persons, giving them human feelings or attributes ('This fell sergeant Death is swift in his arrest').

Images carry powerful significance far deeper than their surface meanings. They enrich particular moments or moods ('O that this too too solid flesh would melt / Thaw and resolve itself into a dew'), and provide insight into character (Hamlet dismisses Osric as a 'water-fly'). Clusters of images, repeated in different forms, embody and express the preoccupations of the play as they build up a sense of themes and issues. Such image clusters include hunting ('get the wind of', 'French falconers', 'springes to catch woodcock', 'false Danish dogs'); war ('mighty opposites', 'an eye like Mars', 'like sleeping soldiers in the alarm'); and, most notably, corruption and theatre.

Corruption

'Something is rotten in the state of Denmark.' Ever since Caroline Spurgeon's pioneering study of Shakespeare's imagery (see page 90), critics have noted the recurrence in *Hamlet* of image clusters relating to poison, disease and corruption. Spurgeon noted the phrase 'the evil smell of evil deeds', and that the word 'rank', meaning rancid and smelly, occurs in several images. Claudius accuses himself: 'O my offence is rank, it smells to heaven'. Hamlet warns his mother against 'rank corruption, mining all within', and is disgusted at the thought of her with Claudius in 'the rank sweat of an enseamèd bed, stewed in corruption'.

The sense of sickness and corruption is widespread. At the beginning of the play Francisco declares he is 'sick at heart'. The Ghost uses the imagery of disease: 'vile and loathsome crust', 'leperous distilment'. Claudius imagines Hamlet as 'the hectic in my blood' and himself as 'like the owner of a foul disease'. Hamlet taunts Claudius with talk of worms and maggots and how a king 'may go a progress through the guts of a beggar'. He thinks of Claudius as 'this canker of our nature'. In the graveyard scene, with its talk of rotting bodies and pocky corses, Hamlet expresses disgust at the odour of the skull ('And smelt so? Pah!'). Social corruption is implied in images of inner bodily corruption. In the closet scene, Hamlet imagines Claudius' court as 'the ulcerous place'. Watching Fortinbras' army marching to certain death, he uses a similar image of an abscess as he reflects:

> This is th'impostume of much wealth and peace,
> That inward breaks, and shows no cause without
> Why the man dies.   *(Act 4 Scene 4, lines 27–9)*

Theatre

Hamlet is an intensely theatrical play. It richly displays Shakespeare's interest in his own profession as actor and playwright, and the London theatres at the end of the reign of Queen Elizabeth. Obvious examples include the presence of the players, the talk of 'little eyases' (boy actors), and the use of the play-within-a-play to reveal Claudius' guilt. The play resonates with the language and imagery of the theatre: 'play', 'act', 'show', 'perform', 'applaud', 'plot', 'prompted', 'cue', 'fool', 'mutes', 'prologue', 'shape' (costume), 'part'. In Hamlet's first appearance he uses 'actions', 'play' and 'show' as he angrily denies his grief is merely signified in his outward appearance:

> For they are actions that a man might play,
> But I have that within which passes show –
>
> > *(Act 1 Scene 2, lines 84–5)*

Hamlet proposes to 'put an antic disposition on' almost as if it were a costume. When he vows he will remember the Ghost 'whiles memory holds a seat in this distracted globe' the images conjured up include his own head, the world and the Globe Theatre itself, whose flag carried the emblem of Hercules with the world on his back. Similarly, some critics have detected images of the Globe in Hamlet's description to Rosencrantz and Guildenstern of how he sees the world (Act 2 Scene 2, lines 281–5): 'goodly frame', 'promontory' (stage), 'canopy', 'this majestical roof fretted with golden fire' (the painted 'heavens' of the Globe stage). But the notion of acting as pretence may symbolise Hamlet's preoccupation with false appearance. Hamlet (himself a fictional character) is amazed that an actor can weep for a fictional character: 'And all for nothing? For Hecuba!'

Doubling

The critic Frank Kermode sees the play as 'obsessed with doubles of all kinds'. Characters are paired: the two sentries at the play's beginning, Rosencrantz and Guildenstern, Cornelius and Voltemand, two English ambassadors, and two kingly brothers, Claudius and Old Hamlet. There are also structural doublings. Hamlet and Laertes both are students, sons, revengers, opponents. The play-within-a-play reflects the Ghost's tale of murder. Hamlet forces his mother to look on two portraits. Laertes, already blessed by his father, is blessed again:

> A double blessing is a double grace   *(Act 1 Scene 3, line 53)*

The play's preoccupation with false appearance has also been claimed as 'doubling'. Duplicity runs through the play as characters pretend to be what they are not. Claudius hides his guilty secret behind an outward show of integrity. Hamlet puts on 'an antic disposition'. Polonius, after telling Laertes not to be false to any man, sets a spy on him. Hamlet viciously accuses Ophelia:

> God hath given you one face and you make yourselves
> another.   *(Act 3 Scene 1, lines 137–8)*

The language of Hamlet strikingly displays doubling. It appears throughout the play in repetition of words and phrases. Sometimes the doubled words occur immediately: 'Tush tush', 'Speak, speak', 'This too too solid flesh', 'To be or not to be' and so on. Polonius seems to say everything twice: 'You have me, have you not?' Most commonly the doubling is achieved by means of the simple conjunction 'and'. When Laertes asks Claudius for permission to return to France, he uses 'leave and favour', 'thoughts and wishes', 'leave and pardon'.

Hamlet contains around 250 examples of such 'doublings'. The critic Harley Granville-Barker claims that Shakespeare had an 'extraordinary fondness' for this doubling device, and Frank Kermode claims that it seems to be the 'very essence' of the play. A special type of such doubling is known as *hendiadys* (pronounced 'hen-die-a-dees'), a technical term meaning 'one through two'. Here, the two words express a single idea. They duplicate the sense rather than amplify or modify each other, as these few examples show:

food and diet	cheer and comfort	pith and marrow
book and volume	grace and mercy	lecture and advice
duty and obedience	heat and flame	fire and spark
flash and outbreak	native and indued	strange and odd

This tendency to use two words when one would be sufficient to convey meaning contributes to dramatic effect. It lengthens the play, adding to the sense of delay. In its suggestion of 'one through two' it echoes the play's concern with marriage and incest (the union of separate selves). Some critics claim that these doublings contain tension or strain, and help create the sense of unease and mystery in the play. How far those claims are valid is a matter of debate, but there is no doubt that doubling is a major feature of the language of *Hamlet*.

Repetition

Doubling is a special case of the repetitions that run through the play. The language is given great dramatic force as repeated words, phrases, rhythms and sounds add to the emotional intensity of a moment or scene, heightening theatrical effect. Repetition may consist of single words:

> Oh horrible, oh horrible, most horrible!   *(Act 1 Scene 5, line 80)*
> O villain, villain, smiling damnèd villain!
> *(Act 1 Scene 5, line 106)*

At other times repetitions recur within the structure of a speech, for example as Horatio challenges the Ghost:

> If thou hast any sound or use of voice,
> Speak to me.
> If there be any good thing to be done
> That may to thee do ease, and grace to me,
> Speak to me.
> If thou art privy to thy country's fate,
> Which happily foreknowing may avoid,
> Oh speak.
> Or if thou hast uphoarded in thy life
> Extorted treasure in the womb of earth,

For which they say you spirits oft walk in death,
Speak of it. Stay and speak!   *(Act 1 Scene 1, lines 128–39)*

A similar structural repetition occurs in dialogue, as between Hamlet and his mother (where the style of rapidly alternating single lines is known as *stichomythia*):

GERTRUDE Hamlet, thou hast thy father much offended.
HAMLET Mother, you have my father much offended.
GERTRUDE Come, come, you answer with an idle tongue.
HAMLET Go, go, you question with a wicked tongue.
                              (Act 3 Scene 4, lines 9–12)

Repetition also occurs in rhyme, but is used to achieve different effects. The use of rhyme in the play-within-a-play emphasises its archaic nature because at the time Shakespeare wrote *Hamlet* such emphatic rhyming was the mark of an old-fashioned style. Elsewhere, a rhyming couplet is sometimes used to give a distinctive ending to an episode or scene:

The play's the thing
Wherein I'll catch the conscience of the king.
                              (Act 2 Scene 2, lines 557–8)

Lists

One of Shakespeare's favourite language methods is to accumulate words or phrases rather like a list. He had learned the technique as a schoolboy in Stratford-upon-Avon, and his skill in knowing how to use lists dramatically is evident in the many examples in *Hamlet*. He intensifies and varies description, atmosphere and argument as he 'piles up' item on item, incident on incident. Sometimes the list comprises only single words, as in Polonius' classifications of plays ('tragedy, comedy, history, pastoral'), or Hamlet's vehement description of Claudius:

Bloody, bawdy villain!
Remorseless, treacherous, lecherous, kindless villain!
                              (Act 2 Scene 2, lines 532–3)

More often each item in the list is given in some detail. Polonius lists the moral guidelines for Laertes' behaviour ('And these few precepts in thy memory / look thou character ...'). Ophelia catalogues Hamlet's princely characteristics ('Oh what a noble mind is here o'erthrown ...'). Claudius makes a veritable inventory of the battalions of sorrows that beset him ('First, her father slain; / Next, your son gone ...'). Other notable examples include those beginning:

'Tis not alone my inky cloak, good mother
(Act 1 Scene 2, lines 77–82)
For who would bear the whips and scorns of time
(Act 3 Scene 1, lines 70–4)
So shall you hear / Of carnal, bloody, and unnatural acts
(Act 5 Scene 2, lines 359–64)

Such lists add to the force of argument, enrich atmosphere, amplify meaning and provide extra dimensions of character. In addition, they provide opportunities for actors to vary their delivery. In speaking, a character usually seeks to give each 'item' a distinctiveness in emphasis and emotional tone, and sometimes an accompanying action and expression.

Verse and prose

In Shakespeare's time, audiences expected actors in tragedies to speak in verse. The poetic style was thought to be particularly suitable for kings, great affairs of state, tragic themes and moments of high dramatic or emotional intensity. Much of the language of *Hamlet* is blank verse: unrhymed verse written in iambic pentameter. It is conventional to define iambic pentameter as a rhythm or metre in which each line has five stressed syllables (/) alternating with five unstressed syllables (×):

$$\times \quad / \quad \times \quad / \quad \times \quad / \quad \times \quad / \quad \times \quad /$$
But die thy thoughts when thy first lord is dead

At school, Shakespeare had learned the definition of iambic pentameter. In Greek, *penta* means 'five', and *iamb* means a 'foot' of two syllables, the first unstressed, the second stressed (as in the pronunciation of 'alas': aLAS). Shakespeare practised writing in that metre, and his early plays, such as *Titus Andronicus* and *Richard III* tend to be very regular in rhythm (de-DUM de-DUM de-DUM de-DUM de-DUM), with each line 'end-stopped' (making sense on its own).

By the time he wrote *Hamlet*, Shakespeare had become much more flexible and experimental in his use of iambic pentameter. End-stopped lines are less frequent. There is greater use of *enjambement* (running on), where one line flows on into the next, seemingly with little or no pause. The 'five-beat' rhythm is less obviously prominent, though usually still present. Lines can have more or fewer than ten syllables. Actors have much discretion in how to deliver the lines; they can pause or emphasise to avoid mechanical or clockwork-sounding speech. The opening lines of the play's most famous soliloquy exemplifies the freedom Shakespeare offers to actors. The many possible different ways of delivery can each be equally valid and dramatically effective:

> To be, or not to be, that is the question –
> Whether 'tis nobler in the mind to suffer
> The slings and arrows of outrageous fortune
>
> *(Act 3 Scene 1, lines 56–8)*

Each line has eleven syllables, and line 57 runs on to line 58. The actor has opportunities to break up a regular iambic pentameter rhythm, for example by stressing 'or', 'is' or 'the' in line 56. It is therefore appropriate when studying, watching or acting in *Hamlet*, not to attempt to apply a rigid rule about how the verse should be spoken. Shakespeare used the convention of iambic pentameter, but he did not adhere to it slavishly. He knew 'the rules', but he was not afraid to break them to suit his dramatic purpose, and the regularities and disjunctions in iambic pentameter provide clues to how to play the lines. No one knows for sure just how the lines were delivered on Shakespeare's own stage, but today actors gratefully seize upon the opportunities Shakespeare's language offers to make thrilling theatre that remains true to the spirit of the play.

Verse or prose?

Just under three-quarters of the play is in verse, just over one-quarter in prose. How did Shakespeare decide whether to write in verse or prose? One answer is that he followed theatrical convention. Prose was traditionally used by 'mad', comic and low-status characters. Aristocrats spoke verse. In *Hamlet*, context needs to be taken into account in judging why characters use prose or verse. The players (low status) speak verse in the Pyrrhus and Gonzago episodes because they are playing aristocratic characters. Hamlet and Ophelia (high status) express their madness in prose.

Another consideration is that verse is more suitable than prose to moments of high dramatic or emotional intensity. So 'serious' scenes are likely to be in verse, 'comic' episodes in prose. But Shakespeare was never afraid to break a rule or convention. Hamlet's 'What a piece of work is a man' is in prose, but it has all the fine qualities claimed for poetry.

Soliloquy

Through soliloquy, Shakespeare enables the audience to gain direct experience of Hamlet's inner world. A soliloquy is a kind of internal debate spoken by a character who is alone on stage, or believes himself to be alone. It is a dramatic convention that a soliloquy reveals the character's true thoughts and feelings. In all his soliloquies, Hamlet explores the contradictions facing him, giving the impression of a man discovering what he thinks as he speaks. Every actor playing Hamlet decides whether to speak none, part, or all of each of his soliloquies directly to the audience.

Antithesis

Antithesis is the opposition of words or phrases against each other, as in 'To be or not to be'; 'I must be cruel only to be kind'; 'Be thou a spirit of health or goblin damned'. This setting of the word against the word ('To be' versus 'not to be'; 'cruel' versus 'kind') is one of Shakespeare's favourite language devices. He uses it extensively in all his plays. Why? Because antithesis powerfully expresses conflict through its use of opposites, and conflict is the essence of all drama. In *Hamlet*, conflict occurs in many forms. Claudius versus Hamlet, revenge versus justice, appearance versus reality, son versus mother, and so on. Antithesis intensifies that sense of conflict, and embodies its different forms.

For example, Claudius' long list of antitheses in his first speech suggest a man attempting to balance conflicting emotions and values (see page 8). Later, Claudius uses an image full of antitheses to acknowledge that a prostitute's use of make-up is similar to how he hypocritically conceals his evil deed behind a mask:

> The harlot's cheek, beautied with plastering art,
> Is not more ugly to the thing that helps it
> Than is my deed to my most painted word.
>
> *(Act 3 Scene 1, lines 51–3)*

Laertes' passionate desire for revenge on Hamlet ('To cut his throat i'th'church') is given additional emotional power by the opposition of the bloodiness of the action with the sanctity of the holy place. In the very last moments of the play, Fortinbras opposes the appropriateness of dead bodies on the battlefield ('field') with their inappropriateness in a court ('here'), and also hints at the corruption that has led to such disaster at Elsinore:

> Such a sight as this
> Becomes the field, but here shows much amiss.
>
> *(Act 5 Scene 2, lines 380–1)*

Critical approaches

Traditional criticism

Hamlet has not always appealed to all critics. In 1748 the French writer Voltaire mockingly dismissed both the play and Shakespeare:

> A coarse and barbarous piece, which would not be tolerated by the basest rabble in France or Italy. Hamlet goes mad in the second act, and his mistress goes mad in the third; the Prince kills his mistress's father, supposing him to be a rat, and the heroine throws herself into the river … one would think that this work was the fruit of the imagination of a drunken savage.

Some critics have been more interested in reading the play, rather than seeing it in the theatre. Two major nineteenth-century critics, whilst praising *Hamlet* on the page, were sceptical about stage performance. Charles Lamb was sure that Hamlet's 'profound sorrows' could not be portrayed by 'a gesticulating actor, who comes and mouths them out before an audience'. William Hazlitt claimed 'We do not like to see our author's plays acted, and least of all, *Hamlet*. There is no play that suffers so much from being transferred to the stage.'

But whatever the attitude of critics to 'page versus stage', it is possible to detect certain trends in critical approaches to *Hamlet*. Doctor Samuel Johnson, perhaps the greatest of the eighteenth-century critics, praised *Hamlet* for its 'variety':

> The incidents are so numerous … the scenes are interchangeably diversified with merriment and solemnity … new characters appear from time to time … every personage produces the effect intended …

Although later critics echoed Johnson's emphasis on the play's variety, they increasingly focused their attention on Hamlet, often treating him as a real person. From the late eighteenth century, through the nineteenth, and well into the twentieth, criticism mainly centred on character, especially Hamlet's. Among the multitude of questions raised about his character, one obsesses nearly all such critics: why did Hamlet delay taking revenge on Claudius?

At the end of the eighteenth century, the great German poet and playwright Goethe wrote of Hamlet's 'lovely, pure, noble and most moral nature'. Goethe viewed Hamlet as a delicate and tender prince whose soul was unfit to meet the demands for action laid upon it. He saw Hamlet as an idealist trapped in a world demanding action, and embittered by his inability to change things.

Goethe symbolised Hamlet as an oak tree planted in a costly vase. The tree grows, and shatters the vase to fragments. That Romantic image of an individual destroyed by his own powerful inner life, is reflected in much nineteenth-century criticism, which casts Hamlet as a tragic hero of hesitation. Alienated from the world in which he finds himself, he is a suffering, spiritual man whose sensitive nature prevents him taking revenge. For William Hazlitt in 1817, Hamlet 'is not a character marked by strength of will or even of passion, but by refinement of thought and sentiment ... his powers of action have been eaten up by thought'. Hazlitt's view of Hamlet preferring thinking over action is shared by Samuel Taylor Coleridge, writing in 1827:

> Hamlet's character is the prevalence of the abstracting and generalising habit over the practical. He does not want [lack] courage, skill, will, or opportunity; but every incident sets him thinking.

Both critics identify themselves with the character under their scrutiny: 'I have a smack of Hamlet myself, if I may say so' (Coleridge), 'It is we who are Hamlet' (Hazlitt). That overt identification reveals a characteristic of all criticism: it cannot be fully objective, but is written from a particular point of view, by a writer whose interests, attitudes and beliefs inevitably shape what he writes. Just as Shakespeare was influenced by the culture of his time, so too is every critic.

The critic with whom the expression 'character study' is most associated is A C Bradley. Around 100 years ago, Bradley delivered a course of lectures at Oxford University which were published in 1904 as *Shakespearean Tragedy*. The book has never been out of print, and Bradley's approach has been hugely influential. It expresses the spirit of much nineteenth-century criticism, and it determined the form of the majority of criticism for a good deal of the twentieth century.

Bradley talks of the characters in *Hamlet* as if they were real human beings existing in worlds recognisable to modern readers. He identifies the unique desires and motives which give Hamlet, Claudius, Gertrude and Ophelia their particular personalities, and which evoke feelings of admiration or disapproval in the audience. Assuming that each character experiences familiar human emotions and thoughts, Bradley's presentation of conflict in *Hamlet* (and the three other tragedies he considers, *Macbeth*, *Othello*, *King Lear*) is primarily that within the individual, an inward struggle. He sees each hero in Shakespeare's tragedies struggling with circumstances and fate, and afflicted with a fatal flaw which causes the tragedy:

> a marked one-sidedness, a predisposition in some particular direction; a total incapacity, in certain circumstances, of resisting the force which draws in this direction; a fatal tendency to identify the whole being with one interest, object, passion or habit of mind. This, it would seem, is, for Shakespeare, the fundamental tragic trait ... some marked imperfection or defect: irresolution, precipitancy, pride, credulousness, excessive simplicity, excessive susceptibility to sexual emotions and the like ... these contribute decisively to the conflict and catastrophe.

This notion of a tragic flaw or *harmatia* is expressed by Hamlet himself, who sees 'the stamp of one defect' in a man leading to his corruption and downfall:

> So, oft it chances in particular men,
> That for some vicious mole of nature in them,
> ...
> His virtues else be they as pure as grace,
> As infinite as man shall undergo,
> Shall in the general censure take corruption
> From that particular fault.   *(Act 1 Scene 4, lines 23–36)*

Bradley's view of Hamlet's 'particular fault' which corrupts his 'virtues' is that he suffers from an excess of melancholy. Hamlet's delay in exacting revenge is a symptom of his melancholy, his disgust for life. That morbid, depressed condition is brought about by what Hamlet sees as his mother's lustful nature and the undue speed with which she married Claudius so shortly after her first husband's death. The nervous shock brought about by her remarriage paralyses Hamlet, rendering him incapable of decisive action.

Bradley's character approach has been much criticised. For example, Hamlet has more than 'one interest, object, passion or habit of mind' (see quotation on page 87). The 'flaw' which contributes towards the tragedy includes melancholy, hatred of Claudius, incapacity to act, over-thoughtfulness. No single formula can sum up Hamlet's complex, divided nature.

Bradley's discussion of *Hamlet* reveals a conception of tragedy which held sway over much criticism through the twentieth century. He views tragedy as mystical and indescribable: 'piteous, fearful ... a painful mystery', which paradoxically, after catastrophe, results in order and unity. Although the tragedies present conflict and waste, evil is eventually overcome. A tragedy's end may not be happy, but it promises something better ahead. For Bradley, virtue and good triumph over suffering, adversity and death itself. He comments on Hamlet's death:

> Fate descends upon his enemies, and his mother, and himself. But he is not left in utter defeat. Not only is his task at last accomplished, but Shakespeare seems to have decided that his hero should exhibit in his latest hour all the glorious power and all the nobility and sweetness of his nature.

This quotation reveals that Bradley's approach encourages judgement of the moral qualities of characters. He saw Hamlet as good, and accepts the descriptions of him by Ophelia ('noble mind', 'th'expectancy and rose of the fair state') and Fortinbras ('for he was likely, had he been put upon, to have proved most royal'). That tendency to judge Hamlet has been followed by many twentieth-century critics, though with different evaluations. Some see him as noble and heroic, others accept Hamlet's own evaluation of himself as 'proud, revengeful, ambitious'.

Today, many critics are sceptical of the optimism of Bradley's interpretation of tragedy, and are uneasy about the whole business of making moral judgements on stage characters. But all through the twentieth century, Bradley exercised a major influence over the study of *Hamlet*. Before considering criticism that radically departs from or rejects his approach, it is helpful to identify some of the major landmarks of traditional criticism. There is of course great variation among the critics who might be called 'traditional', but in general they share certain assumptions:

- a concentration on Hamlet's character, especially what might be his 'tragic flaw'
- a reluctance to address political and social aspects of the play
- a stress on supernatural and mysterious explanations ('fate', 'divine will', etc.)
- an assumption of coherence and unity in the play, and some kind of harmony at its end
- readings which do not challenge existing social structures
- a rejection of 'theory' as providing ways to understand *Hamlet*
- a claim to objectivity, free from ideological bias

Even critics who are usually associated with opening up new approaches to *Hamlet* can be seen to be working within these assumptions. For example, T S Eliot was critical of Shakespeare's achievement, claiming that *Hamlet* was 'full of some stuff that the writer could not drag to light, contemplate, or manipulate into art'. Eliot judged the play an artistic failure, but his judgement can be seen to be rooted in character study. In Eliot's view, Hamlet's disgust is excessive: Gertrude's behaviour is insufficient to justify his emotional condemnation of her.

Similarly, L C Knights, whose essay 'How Many Children Had Lady Macbeth?' famously mocked Bradley's emphasis on character, was himself much concerned with character. Although he argued that study of Shakespeare's plays should focus on poetry and language, his criticism of *Hamlet* is very much a moral reading, asserting that Hamlet 'cannot break out of the closed circle of loathing and self-contempt'.

The same contradiction is found in G Wilson Knight, whose best-known book is *The Wheel of Fire*. Wilson Knight also urged that Shakespeare's plays should be read as dramatic poems, and his concern was for structures, themes and images. But he too is severely judgemental of character, seeing Hamlet as 'an ambassador of death', affecting other characters like a 'blighting disease'. Wilson Knight asserts that the Ghost is 'devilish', and Claudius is a man with 'a host of good qualities', ruling a healthy world that Hamlet's 'diseased consciousness' cruelly destroys. For Wilson Knight, Hamlet is 'inhuman', 'taking delight in cruelty', 'a poison', 'an element of evil in the state of Denmark'.

Other studies which opened up new critical perspectives on the play also share the assumptions listed above. Caroline Spurgeon, in *Shakespeare's Imagery and What it Tells Us*, identified image-clusters as a dominant feature of the plays. She counted the number of times such image-clusters occurred, and argued that they determined the distinctive atmosphere of a play. In *Hamlet*, the recurring images ('iterative imagery') of disease and corruption help establish the atmosphere that 'Something is rotten in the state of Denmark.' Spurgeon claims that the distinctive atmosphere of the play is

> partly due to the number of images of sickness, disease, or blemish of the body … the idea of an ulcer or tumour, as descriptive of the unwholesome condition of Denmark morally, is, on the whole, the dominating one.

John Dover Wilson's imagination was fired by a very practical problem: why did Claudius not respond to the dumb show which portrayed his crime? Dover Wilson was much concerned with the context of the times, and how the court of Denmark reflects that of Queen Elizabeth (see pages 64–8). Nonetheless, his criticism is also much influenced by Bradley: 'The character of the Prince is, of course, the central mystery'. Unlike T S Eliot, Dover Wilson accepts that Gertrude's incest was, for an Elizabethan audience, sufficient cause for Hamlet's morbidity. He claims that Shakespeare asks every spectator, every reader, to sympathise with Hamlet even though

> Shakespeare never lets us forget he (Hamlet) is a failure, or that he has failed through weakness of character

Harold Bloom is the most recent critic to write in the tradition of Bradley's character criticism. *In Shakespeare: The Invention of the Human* (1999), Bloom argues that Shakespeare's characters provided the self-reflexive models by which human beings first acquired selves to reflect on (or to put it more simply, Shakespeare's characters first showed us how to think about ourselves). That enormous claim about the origin of our subjectivity is disputed by almost all scholars. The majority of modern critics are dismissive of Bloom's character study approach as gushing and exaggerated, for example when he describes Hamlet as 'Shakespeare's ideal son', or as 'a villain, cold, murderous, solipsistic, nihilistic, manipulative', or as 'the most aware and knowing figure ever conceived'. Bloom provides many thought-provoking descriptions of Hamlet's many characteristics, but perhaps his most telling remark is:

> categorising Hamlet is virtually impossible . . . it is very
> difficult to generalise about Hamlet, because every observation
> will have to admit its opposite.

Modern criticism

Throughout the second half of the twentieth century and in the twenty-first, critical approaches to Shakespeare have radically challenged the traditional approaches described above. New critical approaches argue that traditional interpretations, with their focus on character, are too individualistic. Further, their detachment from the real world makes them elitist, sexist and apolitical.

Modern radical criticism asserts that traditional criticism divorces literary, dramatic and aesthetic matters from their social context. So in modern criticism the search for what is rotten in the state of Denmark shifts from what is wrong with individuals to focus on social and material conditions: the focus shifts from Hamlet to Denmark. Traditional approaches are seen as concentrating on personal feelings and ignoring history and society. They are criticised for taking a fatalistic view of human existence, for giving prominence to supernatural explanations, and implying that men and women are powerless to resist injustice, because despair and violence are inevitable.

Like traditional criticism, contemporary perspectives include many different approaches but share common features. Modern criticism:

- is sceptical of 'character' approaches (but often uses them!);
- concentrates on political, social and economic factors (arguing that these factors determine Shakespeare's creativity and audiences' and critics' interpretations);

- plays down or rejects supernatural and mysterious explanations;
- identifies contradictions, fragmentation and disunity in the plays;
- questions the possibility of 'happy' or 'hopeful' endings;
- produces readings that are subversive of existing social structures;
- identifies how the plays express the interests of dominant groups – most obviously, rich and powerful males;
- insists that 'theory' is essential to produce valid readings;
- often expresses its commitment (for example, to feminism, or equality, or political change);
- argues all readings are political or ideological readings (and that traditional criticism falsely claims to be objective).

Political criticism

Almost at the end of the play, Horatio says farewell to the dead Hamlet:

> Now cracks a noble heart. Good night sweet prince,
> And flights of angels sing thee to thy rest. –
>
> *(Act 5 Scene 2, lines 338–9)*

Traditional criticism uses these two lines in discussions of Hamlet's nature, often emphasising the description of him as 'sweet prince'. In contrast, political criticism gives all three of Horatio's lines:

> Now cracks a noble heart. Good night sweet prince,
> And flights of angels sing thee to thy rest. –
> Why does the drum come hither?   *(Act 5 Scene 2, lines 338–40)*

For any political critic, the final line is crucial: 'Why does the drum come hither?' Political reality breaks in on religious thoughts as Fortinbras' drum is heard, signalling that a new ruler will shortly take over Denmark. For the political critic, that transfer of power (sometimes enacted as a violent coup, as, for example, in Kenneth Branagh's film) deserves more critical attention than Hamlet's personality or the appealing imagery of flights of angels carrying Hamlet. Political criticism is sceptical of productions which cut Fortinbras. To remove Fortinbras from the play is to reduce its political implications and impact, and to lose the contrast with Hamlet as another revenging son.

So a political interpretation sets Hamlet's personal agony in the context of a world of *realpolitik* (politics concerned only with keeping power, without regard for ethical principles): the threatened Norwegian invasion, busy diplomatic activity, and the intrigue of the court. But the feature that runs through virtually all political approaches is the assumption that *Hamlet* is best studied as a play about a society in the process of change. Denmark has moved from the stability of feudal chivalry to a troubled and unsettled world. In these changed times Hamlet finds himself adrift and powerless, unable to rely on older certainties. There are no longer clear answers to the questions that afflict him: revenge, suicide, the nature of ghosts, salvation. For example, the German playwright Bertolt Brecht saw the play set at a 'fracture point' of society, between an older medieval feudal world and a Protestant one which rules out revenge. Brecht argues that at the Protestant University of Wittenberg Hamlet has learned to reject feudal notions of revenge and to use instead reason and conscience.

Brecht wrote a scene for actors to rehearse in which Hamlet, on his voyage to England, learns that a peace treaty has been signed, in which Denmark gives up some territory, and in exchange Norway agrees to buy Danish fish. Hamlet approves the change from war to peace: 'Blood doesn't smell good any more'. Brecht's point is that Hamlet lives at a time of change, from a feudal world to a modern one, and so can exercise choice. But Brecht, like all political critics, cannot avoid attention to character, as shown in his verse describing Hamlet:

> Here is the body, puffy and inert,
> Where we can trace the virus of the mind.
> How lost he seems among his steel-clad kind
> This introspective sponger in a shirt.

The most notable early challenge to traditional criticism was made by the Polish critic Jan Kott. He fought with the Polish army and underground movement against the Nazis in the Second World War, and had direct experience of the suffering and terror caused by Stalinist repression in Poland in the years after the war. Kott's book *Shakespeare Our Contemporary* saw parallels between the violence and cruelty of the modern world and the worlds of tyranny and despair that Shakespeare depicted in his tragedies.

Kott argues that history, rather than fate or the gods, is the cause of tragedy. He uses the image of 'the Grand Mechanism' of history: a great staircase up which characters tread to their doom, each step 'marked by murder, perfidy, treachery'. It does not matter if a character is good or bad, history will overwhelm them. Characters have little or no power over their lives, but are swept aside by inevitable social and historical forces beyond their control.

In this grim scenario of history, Kott sees *Hamlet* as a fable about totalitarian tyranny: 'Elsinore's a prison camp'. Hamlet is not a Romantic character, but a despairing modern man, and Fortinbras is 'the man of the strong arm' who, with historic inevitability, takes over at the end. The title of Kott's book claims that Shakespeare reflects the same bleak modern view of human history and humanity as Kott himself:

> The genius of *Hamlet* consists in the fact that the play can serve as a mirror. An ideal Hamlet would be one most true to Shakespeare and most modern at the same time ... Hamlet is like a sponge. Unless produced in a stylised or antiquarian fashion, it immediately absorbs all the problems of our time.

Kott has been much criticised by later critics, but he still exercises a powerful influence. He is acknowledged by the director Michael Almereyda as the inspiration for his film of *Hamlet* set in the business corporation climate of contemporary New York (see page 128). Kott can be seen as the forerunner of new critical approaches which focus on the social and political contexts and causes of tragedy. For example, J W Lever in *The Tragedy of State* firmly rejects the focus on the tragic hero in favour of concentrating on the society in which he exists. For Lever, tragedy

> is not primarily treatments of characters with a so-called 'fatal flaw', whose downfall is brought about by the decree of just if inscrutable powers ... the fundamental flaw is in the world they inhabit: in the political state, the social order it upholds ...

In such a view, Hamlet's political powerlessness and alienation springs from the condition of society itself. For political critics, Denmark is very much a prison. It is a closed and secretive world where characters conceal their motives and purposes. Everyone practises deception. Hamlet puts on 'an antic disposition'. Polonius advises Reynaldo to 'put on' any falsehoods as he spies on Laertes. The Players symbolise pretence, and Claudius guiltily reveals his deceit in his response to Polonius laying a trap for Hamlet with his daughter as bait. Polonius urges Ophelia to read a book to 'colour' her loneliness, and comments:

POLONIUS 'Tis too much proved, that with devotion's visage,
    And pious action, we do sugar o'er
    The devil himself.
CLAUDIUS (*Aside*)   Oh, 'tis too true.
    How smart a lash that speech doth give my conscience!
    The harlot's cheek, beautied with plastering art,
    Is not more ugly to the thing that helps it
    Than is my deed to my most painted word.
                          (Act 3 Scene 1, lines 47–53)

In the closing decades of the twentieth century two major schools of political criticism emerged: new historicism (largely American), and cultural materialism (largely British). Their assumptions are virtually the same, but cultural materialism is more concerned with today's world, whereas new historicism focuses on the Elizabethan and Jacobean period.

For most students, it is probably best not to attempt too closely to pigeonhole different types of political criticism. It is more helpful to think of them as sharing a way of reading tragedy that argues that culture (e.g. drama) and materialism (e.g. economic factors) are always related. Interpretations of the tragedies are shaped by the economic, political and ideological (belief) systems of the times, as the context section illustrates (pages 55–73). The following examples show different forms of political criticism.

Stephen Greenblatt asserts that in Shakespeare's England the authorities permitted tragedies to be performed even if they criticised the state, because the effect was to contain and reduce such criticism. After all, the tragedies end with the challenges to authority overcome, and with the same hierarchical system firmly in place. Only the people in the hierarchy have changed. Fortinbras becomes the new, even more powerful ruler of Denmark at the end of *Hamlet*.

Leonard Tennenhouse argues that political ideas are embodied in Hamlet in different images of power. He draws heavily on the theories of the French philosopher Michel Foucault, which assert that political power in a state is maintained through ritual displays and spectacles of punishment. Tennenhouse's complex argument asserts that the play-within-a-play is Hamlet's (unsuccessful) attempt at creating such ritual and spectacle in order 'to locate and purge a corrupt element within the aristocratic body'. Assessing the rival claims to power of Hamlet and Claudius, Tennenhouse writes:

> Hamlet's claim to power derives from his position as son in a patrilinear system as well as from 'popular support'. It is this support which Claudius consistently lacks and which, at the same time, prevents him from moving openly against Hamlet.

The Marxist critic Victor Kiernan attempts to root the tragedies squarely in Shakespeare's own experience of life in Elizabethan and Jacobean England. He claims that Shakespeare's concern was for the poor, whose toil and suffering pays for the pleasures and follies of the rich. For Kiernan, Hamlet is 'Shakespeare's spokesman for common humanity ... aware of hardship and exploitation in the life around him'. He sees in Hamlet's 'O what a rogue and peasant slave am I' soliloquy 'a reminder of how English ploughmen were being degraded into a dispirited race of hired labourers'.

Other critics focus on revenge and justice, seeing them as socially determined. Here, the Ghost's order to revenge is interpreted as a political statement as much as a personal or religious command. Such critics point out how Shakespeare displays the older revenge values and passions in the Player's Hecuba speech and the 'Gonzago' play. They show how these traditional statements contrast with Hamlet's awareness of the complexity of the task the Ghost has laid upon him. He is a man trying to gain justice in a society where the judges are corrupt, and so becomes the scourge of corruption in the state.

Feminist criticism

Feminism aims to achieve rights and equality for women in social, political and economic life. It challenges sexism: those beliefs and practices which result in the degradation, oppression and subordination of women. Feminist criticism therefore challenges traditional portrayals of women characters as examples of 'virtue' or 'vice'. It rejects 'male ownership' of criticism in which men determined what questions were to be asked of a play, and which answers were acceptable.

Feminism argues that male criticism often neglects, represses or misrepresents female experience, and stereotypes or distorts the woman's point of view. Both Gertrude and Ophelia suffer not only at the hands of the men in the play, but also in the writings of male critics who too often adopt Hamlet's own misogynistic (women-hating) viewpoint. Gertrude becomes the emotional focus of the guilt which taints the state of Denmark. Kenneth Muir calls her a 'moral defective'; T S Eliot sees her as 'negative and insignificant'; and Dover Wilson scapegoats her as a sexually guilty woman.

Claudius, the Ghost and Hamlet all seem obsessed with Gertrude as a sex object. Hamlet's feelings for her are expressed in the demeaning language of sexual disgust: 'Frailty, thy name is woman', 'O most pernicious woman', 'stewed in corruption', etc. Feminist critics point out that much traditional criticism and performance has adopted this male view of Gertrude as a lustful, false woman. Rebecca Smith argues that Gertrude

> has traditionally been played as a sensual, deceitful woman ... but the traditional depiction of Gertrude is a false one, because what her words and actions actually create is a soft, obedient, dependent, unimaginative woman who is caught miserably at the centre of a struggle between two 'mighty opposites' ... she loves both Claudius and Hamlet and their conflict leaves her bewildered and unhappy.

Smith is critical of how film versions (by Kozintsev, Richardson and Olivier) portray Gertrude as 'a vain, self-satisfied woman of strong physical and sexual appetites'. In contrast, by careful examination of what Gertrude actually says and does in the play, Smith arrives at a quite different judgement. She finds nothing that suggests wantonness, and concludes that Gertrude's actions are

> as solicitous and unlascivious as her language ... her words and actions compel one to describe Gertrude as merely a quiet, biddable, careful mother and wife ... a compliant, loving, unimaginative woman whose only concern is pleasing others.

Smith's criticism seems very much in the 'character study' tradition of Bradley. But her emphasis on how film versions construct character is crucial. It insists that Shakespeare's *Hamlet* is a play to be performed, and that actors can create character by filling out the 'silences' in the text with expression, gesture and reaction. Gertrude's lines, like those of every character, are an invitation to interpretation.

Ophelia too is subjected to Hamlet's cruel misogyny. He verbally abuses her in the 'nunnery' scene, and subjects her to obscenities as the court prepares to watch the play. She is dominated by her father and brother, who both seek to control her sexuality. Polonius uses her as an instrument in his spying plot, saying he will 'loose' her to Hamlet, an expression more often used of cattle. To all this she seems meekly compliant, making only one (ironic?) remark to Laertes: 'Do not as some ungracious pastors do ...' (Act 1 Scene 3, lines 47–51).

Feminist critics note that Ophelia's madness is usually presented on stage in a more bizarre and exaggerated fashion than Hamlet's. Elaine Showalter points out that although Ophelia is probably the most frequently illustrated of all Shakespeare's heroines (in painting, literature and popular culture), she is neglected to the point of 'invisibility' in traditional criticism, which treats her as

> an insignificant minor character in the play, touching in her
> weakness and madness, but chiefly interesting, of course, in
> what she tells us about Hamlet.

Showalter's own approach to Ophelia is to study the context of her representation. She interprets how portrayals of Ophelia over the centuries, both on stage and in illustrations, have embodied male attitudes to female sexuality and insanity. For example, in Shakespeare's own time, melancholy was a fashionable pose for men, associated with creativity. In women, the condition was much less positively regarded as madness. Showalter concludes that

> The representation of Ophelia changes independently of
> theories of the meaning of the play or the Prince, for it depends
> on attitudes towards women and madness ... There is no 'true'
> Ophelia for whom feminist criticism must unambiguously

speak, but perhaps only a Cubist Ophelia of multiple perspectives, more than the sum of all her parts.

That insistence on multiple perspectives highlights the way in which male critics and directors alike have accepted Hamlet's viewpoint in creating negative constructions of the two female characters, and of 'women' in general. Feminists challenge such views of women's moral frailty. They focus on how such male judgements are constructed from the power relationships within the families of the play and throughout much of history. In both contexts men dominate women, treating them as little more than property.

It is relevant to feminist criticism that Shakespeare provides little textual evidence on which to construct how the two women relate to each other. Although in the graveyard scene Gertrude declares her hope that Hamlet should have married Ophelia, there is little opportunity to create an impression of female friendship, or a sisterhood of resistance. Before Ophelia's descent into madness, the two women speak to each other only once:

GERTRUDE And for your part Ophelia, I do wish
        That your good beauties be the happy cause
        Of Hamlet's wildness. So shall I hope your virtues
        Will bring him to his wonted way again,
        To both your honours.
OPHELIA   Madam, I wish it may.

(Act 3 Scene 1, lines 38–42)

Some actresses have used this exchange, together with non-verbal actions in other scenes, and their behaviour in the 'mad scenes' as opportunities to establish a closer relationship between the two women than the text seems to suggest. That acknowledgement that the text is a script, to be brought to life on a stage, is most fully realised in the next type of modern critical approach to *Hamlet*: performance criticism.

Performance criticism: the 'afterlife' of *Hamlet*
Performance criticism fully acknowledges that *Hamlet* is a play: a script to be performed by actors to an audience. Performance critics note how much *Hamlet* uses the language of theatre such as 'part',

'show', 'play'. They identify how the concepts of drama are integral to the play, as characters are forced by others to perform roles they have great difficulty in playing:

- Hamlet as revenger ('Revenge his foul and most unnatural murder')
- Ophelia as bait ('walk you here ... Read on this book')
- Gertrude as rebuking mother ('tell him his pranks have been too broad to bear with')
- Polonius as eavesdropper ('How now, a rat? Dead for a ducat')
- the players, awkwardly caught up in someone else's drama

Performance criticism is therefore concerned with the staging of the play in the theatre or on film and video. It is part of what is often called the 'afterlife' of *Hamlet*: what happens to the play after the author has written it. Such criticism vividly reveals the instability of *Hamlet*. The play takes very divergent forms in its afterlife, performed and received very differently at different times. The instability begins with the existence of three versions of the play, the First and Second Quartos and the Folio (see pages 55–6). It is heightened by the way in which directors and actors have created new performances of the play over the centuries.

Hamlet has always been a popular play. With the exception of the 18-year period when all theatres were closed under the Commonwealth (1642–60), it has never been absent from the stage for long. There is even a record of a version acted on a ship off the coast of Sierra Leone in 1608. It has been the inspiration for all kinds of 'offshoots' or adaptations: operas, ballets, novels, parodies, films, paintings, cartoons, advertisements, journalism. Quotations from the play are used in virtually all forms of discourse (Samuel Pepys notes in his diary that he learned by heart the 'To be or not to be' soliloquy). *Hamlet*'s capacity to create an infinity of meanings is evident in its huge cultural legacy. Aspects of it appear in all areas of 'popular' and 'high' culture.

The play has always been a star vehicle for the major actors of each generation. But in every age the text has been cut, altered and added to. For 400 years, since its first performance in 1601, audiences have watched and heard very different versions of *Hamlet*. For example, Fortinbras disappeared totally from stagings between 1732 and 1897.

That tradition still influences productions in the twenty-first century. For some modern audiences the play ends with Hamlet's death: 'the rest is silence'. There is not space to describe the many very different versions, but the example of the famous eighteenth-century actor–manager David Garrick shows there is no such thing as the 'authentic' *Hamlet*.

Garrick was concerned to portray Hamlet as a truly noble prince, and to make the play into what he saw as a genuine tragedy. He therefore cut anything that detracted from a heroic image of Hamlet, and removed what he called 'the rubbish of the fifth act': Ophelia's funeral and the Gravediggers. Garrick's audiences did not hear how Hamlet sent Rosencrantz and Guildenstern to their deaths, or the 'Now might I do it pat' speech, both deemed to be unsuitable to Hamlet's noble nature. Laertes did not poison his sword, nor Claudius the drink. Gertrude died offstage in guilt-ridden insanity, Fortinbras did not appear, and Laertes survived the duel to rule over Denmark jointly with Horatio.

In the nineteenth century many productions presented Romantic interpretations of an intellectual, sensitive prince, unable to sweep swiftly to revenge. Productions attempted to create the illusion of an historically accurate castle of Elsinore (which in practice meant a Victorian conception of such castles). In the twentieth century Hamlet was increasingly portrayed as alienated, and productions tended to abandon attempts at realism. They relied more on bare stages with a minimum of scenery and with scenes flowing swiftly into each other. This might be seen as an attempt to return to the conditions of Shakespeare's own Globe stage, which was not dependent on theatrical illusion.

Gurr and Ichikawa, in *Staging in Shakespeare's Theatres*, give a scene-by-scene account of how *Hamlet* may have been first performed, and suggest how very differently an Elizabethan audience might have responded. For that audience, Laertes and Hamlet leaping into the grave symbolised their damnation as revengers, because the stage grave trap was seen as the gateway to hell. The appearance of Fortinbras at the end of the play, in armour, wearing a helmet, would have a potent effect. Shakespeare's audiences, because of their familiarity with the revenge tradition of drama, would see Fortinbras as the vengeful Ghost of Act I returning to celebrate his victory. For Gurr and Ichikawa *Hamlet* is a play that stresses its own theatricality. It is, to use their term, 'metatheatre': theatre about theatre.

Performance criticism, with its focus on Shakespeare's stagecraft and the semiotics of theatre (signs: words, costumes, gestures, etc.), is a rapidly growing area of study. An early and very influential critic was Harley Granville-Barker, himself a playwright and director. His *Prefaces to Shakespeare: Hamlet* discusses scene-by-scene staging of the play, and is the model for Michael Pennington's *Hamlet: A User's Guide*. Both give detailed prescriptive advice on staging.

Another aspect of performance criticism identifies how the play takes on new meanings and resonances in different places and at different times. Before the collapse of Communism, performances of *Hamlet* offered a subversive political metaphor in Eastern European countries and the Soviet Union (the dictator Stalin had earlier banned the play from all Soviet theatres). Marcellus' line 'Something is rotten in the state of Denmark' was often greeted with applause. In a Romanian production, Elsinore was portrayed as a disintegrating museum, a powerful image that reflected the highly bureaucratised Communist state. In Poland, a production showed Fortinbras entering at the end dressed as a Soviet Commissar. A Moscow staging used a huge moving curtain to conceal and reveal spies and to sweep characters on and off stage to their deaths. In 1960s England, the Royal Shakespeare Company expressed the mood of the times by portraying Hamlet as a baffled student idealist, powerless in a harsh political world.

The widespread availability of films of *Hamlet* on video and DVD (see page 128) has made performance criticism even more significant in the twenty-first century. Film offers valuable opportunities to analyse aspects of performance in different productions: character, relationships, conceptual and interpretive approaches, cuts, settings. It also provides close-ups, tracking shots and cinematic spectacle which cannot be achieved on stage. In the Russian film, Fortinbras' army marches along a real sea coast; in Branagh's film, Claudius' court teems with soldiers and courtiers. Hamlet's face sometimes fills the entire screen, and the actor's expression can heighten the sense of inner turmoil. Film can even suggest moral perspectives, as when Olivier uses high angle shots to look down on Claudius' court as if in moral judgement.

Psychoanalytic criticism

In the twentieth century, psychoanalysis became a major influence on the understanding and interpretation of human behaviour. The founder of psychoanalysis, Sigmund Freud, explained personality as the result of unconscious and irrational desires, repressed memories or wishes, sexuality, fantasy, anxiety and conflict. Freud's theories, together with his stress on early childhood experiences, have strongly influenced criticism and stagings of *Hamlet*.

All the Freudian characteristics noted in the previous paragraph are present in Ernest Jones' book *Oedipus and Hamlet*. Jones refers to Hamlet as 'the sphinx of modern literature', and sees the central enigma as how to explain Hamlet's delay. His 'psychoanalytic solution' is that Hamlet suffers from the Oedipus complex (the desire to kill his father and sleep with his mother). The complex provides the unconscious motive for his delay, not the cowardice, doubts about the Ghost, or wish for Claudius' damnation that Hamlet himself claims. For Jones, 'the heart of the situation' lies in Hamlet's childhood feelings:

> Hamlet had in years gone by, as a child, bitterly resented having had to share his mother's affection, even with his own father, had regarded him as a rival, and had secretly wished him out of the way so that he might enjoy undisputed and undisturbed the monopoly of that affection.

Jones interprets Hamlet's strongly expressed disgust for his mother's behaviour and his delay in killing Claudius as being due to repression of his sexual desire for his mother. Jones asserts that Hamlet cannot bring himself to kill Claudius because Claudius has done precisely what Hamlet himself wanted to do. He has murdered Hamlet's father and married his mother. Hamlet is repressing an unconscious desire to have displaced his father himself.

Jones' book has had a major influence on performance of the play, most famously in Laurence Olivier's 1948 film. Gertrude's bed is a powerful symbolic presence throughout the film, and Hamlet behaves as much like Gertrude's lover as her son. In the first court scene they kiss passionately, and in the closet scene Hamlet seems close to raping his mother. Although for Elizabethans 'closet' merely meant a private room, it has become almost a stage convention to set the scene in Gertrude's bedroom to heighten the Freudian implication that Hamlet secretly sexually desires his mother.

But the Oedipus complex, like all psychoanalytic theories, has obvious weaknesses. It cannot be proved or disproved, and it neglects historical and social factors. When applied to drama, psychoanalytic approaches often impose meaning from theory rather than from the text. Nonetheless, because psychoanalysis is concerned with personal trauma or anxiety and with dysfunctional family relationships, it has obvious appeal in discussions of *Hamlet*.

Postmodern criticism

Postmodern criticism (sometimes called 'deconstruction') is not always easy to understand because it is not centrally concerned with consistency or reasoned argument. It does not accept that one section of the story is necessarily connected to what follows, or that characters relate to each other in meaningful ways. The approach therefore has obvious drawbacks in providing a model for examination students, who are expected to display consistency and reasoned argument in their work.

Postmodern approaches to *Hamlet* are most clearly seen in stage productions. There, you could think of it as simply 'a mixture of styles'. The label 'postmodern' is applied to productions which self-consciously show little regard for consistency in character, or for coherence in telling the story. Characters are dressed in costumes from very different historical periods, and carry both modern and ancient weapons. Ironically, Shakespeare himself has been regarded as a postmodern writer in the way he mixes genres in his plays: comedy (the Gravediggers) with tragedy (the revenge plot).

Postmodernism often revels in the cleverness of its own use of language, and accepts all kinds of anomalies and contradictions in a spirit of playfulness or 'carnival'. It abandons any notion of the organic unity of the play, and rejects the assumption that *Hamlet* possesses clear patterns or themes. Its emphasis on paradox and fragmentation in the text can be seen in James Calderwood's assertion that the style of Hamlet's instruction to Gertrude in Act 3 Scene 4, lines 182–9 ('Not this, by no means ... mad in craft') 'would appear to license contradictions, ambiguities, multiplications of meaning':

> The play resists positive interpretation ... the paradox of
> negation is at its most duplicitous in Hamlet's advice to his
> mother. Here the double negative functions as a conceptual
> eraser of all that follows it. This suggests how tenuous and
> vulnerable language is in the presence of the negative.

Calderwood displays postmodernism's obsession with language. His first five words demonstrate how some critics even deny the possibility of finding meaning in language. They claim that words simply refer to other words, and so any interpretation is endlessly delayed (or 'deferred' as the deconstructionists say). Other critics focus on minor or marginal characters, or on gaps or silences in the play. They claim that these features, previously overlooked as unimportant, reveal significant truths about the play.

Because of such assumptions, postmodern criticism is sometimes described as 'reading against the grain' or, less politely, as 'textual harassment'. Perhaps its most controversial feature is 'the denial of subjectivity': the assertion that human beings (or characters in plays) have no essential identity. That position can be seen in Terry Eagleton's discussion of Hamlet's angry accusation that Rosencrantz and Guildenstern want to 'pluck out the heart of my mystery'. Eagleton writes:

> But the irony of this ... is that there is no heart of the mystery
> to be plucked out. Hamlet has no 'essence' of being
> whatsoever, no inner sanctum to be safeguarded: he is pure
> deferral and diffusion, a hollow void which offers nothing
> determinate to be known.

Organising your responses

The purpose of this section is to help you improve your writing about *Hamlet*. It offers practical guidance on two kinds of tasks: writing about an extract from the play and writing an essay. Whether you are answering an examination question, preparing coursework (term paper), or carrying out research into your own chosen topic, this section will help you organise and present your responses.

In all your writing, there are three vital things to remember:

- *Hamlet* is a play. Although it is usually referred to as a 'text', *Hamlet* is not a book, but a script intended to be acted on a stage. So your writing should demonstrate an awareness of the play in performance as theatre. That means you should always try to read the play with an 'inner eye', thinking about how it could look and sound on stage. By doing so, you will be able to write effectively about Shakespeare's language and dramatic techniques.

- *Hamlet* is not a presentation of 'reality'. It is a dramatic construct in which the playwright, through theatre, engages the emotions and intellect of the audience. The characters and story may persuade an audience to suspend its disbelief for several hours. The audience may identify with the characters, be deeply moved by them, and may think of them as if they are living human beings. However, when you write, a major part of your task is to show how Shakespeare achieves the dramatic effects that so engage the audience. Through discussion of his handling of language, character and plot, your writing reveals how Shakespeare uses themes and ideas, attitudes and values, to give insight into crucial social, moral and political dilemmas of his time – and yours.

- How Shakespeare learned his craft. As a schoolboy, and in his early years as a dramatist, Shakespeare used all kinds of models or frameworks to guide his writing. But he quickly learned how to vary and adapt the models to his own dramatic purposes. This section offers frameworks that you can use to structure your writing. As you use them, follow Shakespeare's example! Adapt them to suit your own writing style and needs.

Writing about an extract

It is an expected part of all Shakespeare study that you should be able to write well about an extract (sometimes called a 'passage') from the play. An extract is usually between 30 and 70 lines long, and you are invited to comment on it. The instructions vary. Sometimes the task is very briefly expressed:

- Write a detailed commentary on the following passage.
- Write about the effect of the extract on your own thoughts and feelings.

At other times a particular focus is specified for your writing:

- With close reference to the language and imagery of the passage, show in what ways it helps to establish important issues in the play.
- Analyse the style and structure of the extract, showing what it contributes to your appreciation of the play's major concerns.

In writing your response, you must of course take account of the precise wording of the task, and ensure you concentrate on each particular point specified. But however the invitation to write about an extract is expressed, it requires you to comment in detail on the language. You should identify and evaluate how the language reveals character, contributes to plot development, offers opportunities for dramatic effect, and embodies crucial concerns of the play as a whole. These 'crucial concerns' are also referred to as the 'themes', or 'issues', or 'preoccupations' of the play.

The framework on page 108 is a guide to how you can write a detailed commentary on an extract. Writing a paragraph on each item will help you bring out the meaning and significance of the extract, and show how Shakespeare achieves his effects.

The framework is followed by two examples. The first, on the opening of the 'closet scene', shows how the paragraphs making up the essay might be written. The second, on Hamlet's 'To be, or not to be' soliloquy, presents how you might make notes to guide your writing of each paragraph. The framework headings (in bold) would not, of course, appear in your essay. They are presented only to help you see how the framework is used.

Paragraph 1: Locate the extract in the play and say who is on stage.
Paragraph 2: State what the extract is about and identify its structure.
Paragraph 3: Identify the mood or atmosphere of the extract.

Paragraphs 4–8:	These paragraphs analyse how
Diction (vocabulary)	Shakespeare achieves his effects. They
Imagery	concentrate on the language of the
Antithesis	extract, showing the dramatic effect of
Repetition	each item, and how the language
Lists	expresses crucial concerns of the play.

Paragraph 9: Staging opportunities
Paragraph 10: Conclusion

Extract 1

POLONIUS He will come straight. Look you lay home to him.   1
    Tell him his pranks have been too broad to bear with,
    And that your grace hath screened and stood between
    Much heat and him. I'll silence me e'en here.
    Pray you be round with him.   5

HAMLET (*Within*) Mother, mother, mother!

GERTRUDE I'll warrant you, fear me not. Withdraw, I hear him coming.

[*Polonius hides himself behind the arras*]

Enter Hamlet

HAMLET Now mother, what's the matter?

GERTRUDE Hamlet, thou hast thy father much offended.

HAMLET Mother, you have my father much offended.   10

GERTRUDE Come, come, you answer with an idle tongue.

HAMLET Go, go, you question with a wicked tongue.

GERTRUDE Why, how now Hamlet?

HAMLET   What's the matter now?

GERTRUDE Have you forgot me?

HAMLET   No by the rood, not so.

    You are the queen, your husband's brother's wife,   15
    And, would it were not so, you are my mother.

GERTRUDE Nay, then I'll set those to you that can speak.

HAMLET Come, come and sit you down, you shall not budge.
    You go not till I set you up a glass
    Where you may see the inmost part of you.   20

GERTRUDE What wilt thou do? thou wilt not murder me?
    Help, help, ho!

POLONIUS (*Behind*) What ho! Help, help, help!

HAMLET (*Draws*) How now, a rat? Dead for a ducat, dead.

Kills Polonius

POLONIUS (*Behind*) Oh, I am slain!

GERTRUDE   Oh me, what hast thou done?   25

HAMLET Nay I know not, is it the king?

GERTRUDE Oh what a rash and bloody deed is this!

HAMLET A bloody deed? Almost as bad, good mother,

    As kill a king and marry with his brother.

GERTRUDE As kill a king?

HAMLET   Ay lady, 'twas my word.   30

[*Lifts up the arras and reveals the body of Polonius*]

    Thou wretched, rash, intruding fool, farewell.

    I took thee for thy better. Take thy fortune.

    Thou find'st to be too busy is some danger. –

    Leave wringing of your hands. Peace! Sit you down

    And let me wring your heart, for so I shall   35

    If it be made of penetrable stuff,

    If damnèd custom have not brazed it so,

    That it be proof and bulwark against sense.

GERTRUDE What have I done, that thou dar'st wag thy tongue

    In noise so rude against me?

HAMLET   Such an act   40

    That blurs the grace and blush of modesty,

    Calls virtue hypocrite, takes off the rose

    From the fair forehead of an innocent love

    And sets a blister there, makes marriage vows

    As false as dicers' oaths. Oh such a deed   45

    As from the body of contraction plucks

    The very soul, and sweet religion makes

    A rhapsody of words. Heaven's face doth glow;

    Yea, this solidity and compound mass,

    With tristful visage as against the doom,   50

    Is thought-sick at the act.

GERTRUDE   Ay me, what act,

    That roars so loud and thunders in the index?

HAMLET Look here upon this picture, and on this,

    The counterfeit presentment of two brothers.

    See what a grace was seated on this brow;   55

Hyperion's curls, the front of Jove himself,
An eye like Mars, to threaten and command;
A station like the herald Mercury,
New-lighted on a heaven-kissing hill;
A combination and a form indeed,   60
Where every god did seem to set his seal
To give the world assurance of a man.
This was your husband. Look you now what follows.
Here is your husband, like a mildewed ear
Blasting his wholesome brother. Have you eyes?   65
Could you on this fair mountain leave to feed
And batten on this moor?   *(Act 3 Scene 4, lines 1–67)*

Paragraph 1: Locate the extract in the play and say who is on stage.

It is shortly after the play-within-a-play has forced Claudius to face up
to his guilt. Hamlet has just refrained from killing the king at prayer,
hoping to kill him at a time which will condemn him to hell. Now
Hamlet is about to confront his mother. Polonius and Gertrude are on
stage, and Polonius, typically concerned with surveillance, plans to
overhear the conversation between mother and son.

Paragraph 2: State what the extract is about and identify its structure.

(Begin with one or two sentences identifying what the extract is about,
followed by several sentences briefly identifying its structure, that is,
the different sections of the extract.)

The extract shows how Polonius finally pays the price for
eavesdropping. It reveals the violent intensity of Hamlet's emotions,
which provoke him to kill Polonius, passionately rebuke his mother,
and compare the noble qualities of his father with the vileness of
Claudius. Its structure is a sequence of events. Polonius tells Gertrude
to rebuke Hamlet for his behaviour, then hides. He is killed by
Hamlet, who suspects it is the king who is hiding. Hamlet vehemently
criticises his mother, then praises his father and condemns Claudius.

Paragraph 3: Identify the mood or atmosphere of the extract.

The scene opens in a mood of anxious or nervous expectation as
Polonius and Gertrude prepare for Hamlet's entry. The rest of the
scene is full of anger and passion as Hamlet rails against his mother,
and, in one abrupt and violent moment, slays Polonius.

Paragraph 4: Diction (vocabulary)

Polonius' language is typical of him. Even though he says he will 'silence' himself, he cannot refrain from adding yet another instruction, ordering Gertrude to speak sharply to Hamlet: 'be round with him.' And yet his 'I'll silence me e'en here' is full of dramatic irony; he will shortly be silenced for ever. Hamlet's language displays the intensity of his feelings towards his mother. It is full of orders: 'Go, go', 'Come, come', 'sit you down', 'Look here'. It also uses many words and phrases that seem to accuse Gertrude, for example 'kill a king', 'marry with his brother', 'blurs', 'blister', 'false', 'thought-sick at the act'.

Paragraph 5: Imagery

Polonius' curious image of Gertrude as a firescreen implies that she has shielded Hamlet from criticism: 'stood between / Much heat and him.' It deepens the impression of how much she cares for him. Hamlet's vivid images convey his extreme emotions. He kills Polonius as 'a rat', thinking he is Claudius. He accuses Gertrude's heart of being armoured ('proof and bulwark') against feeling. He implies she is like a prostitute who was branded on the forehead ('sets a blister there') and that in marrying Claudius she has made religion a meaningless jumble ('rhapsody'). He uses god-like images to compare his father ('Hyperion', 'Jove', 'Mars', 'Mercury') with the corruption and barrenness of Claudius ('mildewed ear', 'moor').

Paragraph 6: Antithesis

The emotional conflict between Gertrude and Hamlet is expressed in all kinds of oppositions. 'Father' is set against 'mother', 'hands' against 'heart', 'virtue' against 'hypocrite', 'rose' against 'blister', 'marriage vows' against 'dicers' oaths', 'Heaven's face' against 'glow' (blush). Hamlet embarks on an extended contrast of the 'grace' of his father with the corruption of Claudius. He probably speaks 'your husband' with utter contempt, and emphasises the antitheses of 'mildewed ear / Blasting his wholesome brother' and 'fair mountain' versus 'moor'.

Paragraph 7: Repetition

Polonius typically repeats his instructions in different ways ('Look you', 'Tell him', 'Pray you') giving the actor the opportunity to bring out the finicky, controlling aspect of his character. Before he appears, Hamlet calls 'Mother, mother, mother', and in his exchanges with his mother, words are repeated which give important emphasis to other preoccupations of the play: 'dead', 'deed', 'king', 'act'. At first Hamlet echoes the form and rhythm of Gertrude's lines, but changes words to express what obsesses and angers him: the familiar 'thou' becomes the more formal 'you', 'thy father' becomes 'my father', and 'idle tongue' becomes 'wicked tongue'. This one-line rapid-fire exchange (known as *stichomythia*) heightens dramatic tension as one line is precisely challenged by its opposite, and Hamlet can charge the changed words with the disgust he feels. The instances of the 'doubling' which pervades the whole play, also intensify both meaning and emotional impact. They give the actor many opportunities to vary how he speaks each pair: 'rash and bloody deed', 'proof and bulwark', 'grace and blush', 'solidity and compound mass', 'roars so loud and thunders', 'threaten and command', 'combination and a form'.

Paragraph 8: Lists

Shakespeare uses another language technique to enable Hamlet to express the violence of his feelings. He lists what causes his emotional distress, piling item upon item to heighten the impact of his words. His catalogue of family relationships is intended to wound his mother deeply: 'You are the queen, your husband's brother's wife, / And, would it were not so, you are my mother.' Other 'lists' which the actor can speak to accumulating but different effect include:

- his description of Polonius: 'wretched, rash, intruding fool'. Spoken increasingly dismissively?
- his long account of Gertrude's offensive 'act' in lines 40–51 which can be spoken as an increasing catalogue of at least eight reprehensible items (from 'blurs the grace' to 'thought-sick at the act'). Spoken with increasing anguish?
- his praise, point by point, of his father's qualities, from 'See what a grace' to 'assurance of a man'. Spoken with developing wonder and admiration? Or with increasing regret at what is now lost?

Paragraph 9: Staging opportunities

Shakespeare set this scene in Gertrude's closet, her private room. But many modern productions follow the example of Laurence Olivier's film and set it in Gertrude's bedroom. This can heighten the Freudian interpretation that Hamlet has an Oedipus complex: he secretly wishes to become his mother's lover. The impression is heightened if he pushes his mother onto her bed at 'sit you down', or if he holds her with increasing force as he speaks his lines condemning her or praising his father. But this is a relatively modern interpretation. Elizabethan audiences were more likely to respond to what was for them a different taboo: the marriage of brother and sister-in-law ('and marry with his brother'). The scene provides many other opportunities for heightened dramatic effect. For example, the stabbing of Polonius can be a prolonged, savage affair, and Hamlet can speak with breathless expectancy or excitement or exultation as he asks 'is it the king?' The scene also offers Gertrude the opportunity to show that for the very first time she suspects what Claudius has done. She can repeat Hamlet's words with incredulity, but with dawning recognition of her new husband's evil act: 'As kill a king?' Use of props can also enhance dramatic impact, where, for example, Hamlet wears his father's picture on a chain about his neck, and Gertrude wears a similar medallion bearing a miniature of Claudius. Hamlet snatching Gertrude's chain forces mother and son into close and tense proximity.

Paragraph 10: Conclusion
In such ways the scene offers many opportunities for different ways of performance. It is also a crucial turning point in the plot, because Polonius' death will tip Ophelia over into madness and turn Laertes into another of the play's revengers. In addition, it reveals fresh aspects of the characters of Gertrude and Hamlet and their relationship. She is at first reprimanding, then fearful, then increasingly puzzled by her son's violent actions and words. He unleashes all his spleen directly on his mother, and in an impulsive moment acts to revenge his father, but mistakenly kills Polonius. Shakespeare thus emphasises the revenge theme of the play and adds extra intensity to its preoccupation with corruption, death and surveillance (Polonius pays the price of constant eavesdropping). Finally, in Polonius' and Hamlet's treatment of Gertrude, Shakespeare again stresses how the play demonstrates gender submission: women are subject to the orders and abuse of men.

Extract 2

To be, or not to be, that is the question –   1
Whether 'tis nobler in the mind to suffer
The slings and arrows of outrageous fortune,
Or to take arms against a sea of troubles,
And by opposing end them. To die, to sleep –   5
No more; and by a sleep to say we end
The heart-ache and the thousand natural shocks
That flesh is heir to – 'tis a consummation
Devoutly to be wished. To die, to sleep –
To sleep, perchance to dream. Ay, there's the rub,   10
For in that sleep of death what dreams may come,
When we have shuffled off this mortal coil,
Must give us pause. There's the respect
That makes calamity of so long life,
For who would bear the whips and scorns of time,   15
Th'oppressor's wrong, the proud man's contumely,
The pangs of disprized love, the law's delay,
The insolence of office, and the spurns
That patient merit of th'unworthy takes,
When he himself might his quietus make   20
With a bare bodkin? Who would fardels bear,
To grunt and sweat under a weary life,
But that the dread of something after death,
The undiscovered country from whose bourn
No traveller returns, puzzles the will,   25
And makes us rather bear those ills we have
Then fly to others that we know not of?
Thus conscience does make cowards of us all,
And thus the native hue of resolution
Is sicklied o'er with the pale cast of thought,   30
And enterprises of great pitch and moment
With this regard their currents turn awry
And lose the name of action. Soft you now,
The fair Ophelia. – Nymph, in thy orisons
Be all my sins remembered.   *(Act 3 Scene 1, lines 56–90)*

Paragraph 1: Locate the extract in the play and say who is on stage.
- towards the midpoint of the play, a turning point for Hamlet

- the Ghost has charged Hamlet to revenge his father's murder. Hamlet has put on an 'antic disposition', and plans to use a play to force Claudius to reveal his guilt
- but Claudius and Polonius are spying on him, using Ophelia as bait
- so although Hamlet thinks he is alone, he is being watched

Paragraph 2: State what the extract is about and identify its structure.
- the most widely accepted interpretation of the soliloquy is that Hamlet is considering whether or not to commit suicide
- the soliloquy has also been interpreted in other ways: Hamlet wondering whether he should kill Claudius; and Hamlet reflecting whether life itself is worth living (a favourite debating topic in Shakespeare's time)
- the soliloquy embodies crucial themes of the play: the concern with death, the afterlife, suffering

The structure of the extract shows Hamlet's mind moving from thought to thought:

- Hamlet first asks himself the question whether or not he should commit suicide
- then he weighs up considerations: 'whether', 'Or', etc.
- he wonders whether the most noble course is to suffer all life's hardships or fight against them
- he sees death as a sleep, but is troubled by what may happen in that sleep of death – he reflects that what stops people committing suicide, in spite of all the oppressions and injustices of life, is fear of the terrors that await the dead
- he concludes that such thinking prevents decisive action
- dramatic effect: the soliloquy creates a reflective tone and heightens the sense of delay

Paragraph 3: Identify the mood or atmosphere of the extract.
- sombre, reflective, like a developing argument
- dejected and pessimistic, expressing despair and disillusion
- the mood reflects themes – the questioning tone of the play, the uncertainty about what to do

Paragraph 4: Diction (vocabulary)
- certain words and phrases contribute to the subject matter and atmosphere (e.g. the sombre tone, the preoccupation with death in 'not to be', 'suffer', 'die', 'heart-ache', 'shocks')

- the different ways of expressing death: 'not to be', 'sleep', 'shuffled off this mortal coil', 'quietus', 'The undiscovered country' are all euphemisms, adding an ominous tone

Paragraph 5: Imagery
- because soliloquy so rich in imagery, can mention only a few examples
- 'slings and arrows of outrageous fortune', 'take arms against a sea of troubles' (confused metaphor? how can you fight the sea?) 'heart-ache and the thousand natural shocks', 'there's the rub', 'shuffled off this mortal coil', 'whips and scorns of time'
- cumulative effect of imagery is of human life as subject to assault
- if time, mention 'the undiscovered country' from which 'no traveller returns'; this description of death suggests that Hamlet has forgotten his encounter with the Ghost

Paragraph 6: Antithesis
- give examples of oppositions: 'To be, or not to be', 'Whether .../Or', 'sleep/dream', 'calamity / long life', 'bear / Then fly', 'conscience/ cowards'
- dramatic effect: contributes to the 'weighing', reflective tone as Hamlet balances alternatives, for and against. The opposition of life versus death: all an extension of first line 'To be, or not to be'
- conveys the intense working of his mind; shows soliloquy as a kind of internal debate

Paragraph 7: Repetition
- give examples of repetition of words (e.g. 'sleep', 'thus', 'bear': 'who would bear ...'; 'Who would fardels bear ...'; 'bear those ills'), phrases, rhythms ('To be', 'to die, to sleep', etc.)
- notice 'doubles' using 'and' (typical of whole play): 'slings and arrows', 'heart-ache and the thousand natural shocks', 'whips and scorns', 'grunt and sweat', 'great pitch and moment'
- dramatic effect: repetition slows up pace (reflective tone), but adds depth and reinforcement of meaning and atmosphere

Paragraph 8: Lists
- use the most obvious list: 'the whips and scorns of time ... the spurns / That patient merit of th'unworthy takes' (lines 15–19)

- seven items give cumulative sense of humanity's burdens
- may refer to Hamlet's own situation – the rough hand he's been dealt, Claudius' oppression and sneering, Ophelia's locking him out, slowness of justice, the slights he feels he endures in the court
- or could be general condemnation of how individual is trapped in society

Paragraph 9: Staging opportunities
- soliloquy: deliver to audience, or self or ...?
- give examples (Olivier, Gibson, Branagh): all intended to display 'inner' Hamlet?
- how might Hamlet enter? Actions throughout?
- how and where do Claudius and Polonius conceal themselves to spy on Hamlet?
- Ophelia remains on stage, but where? and what does she do?
- is Hamlet aware from the start that he is being watched?

Paragraph 10: Conclusion
(Try to find a fresh way of concluding – not just repeating.)
- Hamlet's soliloquies are evidence of Shakespeare's desire to explore/expose Hamlet's inner world
- gives impression of a man discovering what he thinks as he speaks
- reveals character (Hamlet as reflective, agonised, uncertain)
- may be a psychological turning point, midway through the play
- progresses plot (here, it slows up rapid development of plot, reflecting the play itself, which is full of digressions and delay)
- expresses themes (uncertainty, delay, death)
- gives multiple performance opportunities

Reminders

- The framework is only a guide. It will help you to structure your writing. Use the framework for practice on other extracts. Adapt as you feel appropriate. Make it your own.
- Structure your response in paragraphs. Each paragraph makes a particular point and helps build up your argument.
- Focus tightly on the language, especially vocabulary, imagery, antithesis, lists, repetitions.
- Remember that *Hamlet* is a play, a drama intended for performance. The purpose of writing about an extract is to identify how Shakespeare creates dramatic effect. What techniques does he use?
- Try to imagine the action. Visualise the scene in your mind's eye. But remember there can be many valid ways of performing a scene. Offer alternatives. Justify your own preferences by reference to the language.
- Who is on stage? Imagine their interaction. How do 'silent characters' react to what is said?
- Look for the theatrical qualities of the extract. What guides for actors' movement and expressions are given in the language? Comment on any stage directions.
- How might the audience respond? In Elizabethan times? Today? How might you respond as a member of the audience?
- How might the lines be spoken? Tone, emphasis, pace, pauses? Identify shifting moods and registers. Is the verse pattern smooth or broken; flowing or full of hesitations and abrupt turns?
- What is the importance of the extract in the play as a whole? Justify its thematic significance.
- Are there any 'key words'?
- How does the extract develop the plot, reveal character, deepen themes?
- In what ways can the extract be spoken/staged to reflect a particular interpretation?

Writing an essay

As part of your study of *Hamlet* you will be asked to write essays, either under examination conditions or for coursework ('term papers'). Examinations mean that you are under pressure of time, usually having around one hour to prepare and write each essay. Coursework means that you have much longer to think about and produce your essay. But, whatever the type of essay, each will require you to develop an argument about a particular aspect of *Hamlet*.

The essays you write on *Hamlet* require that you set out your thoughts on a particular aspect of the play, using evidence from the text. The people who read your essays (examiners, teachers, lecturers) will have certain expectations of your writing. In each essay they will expect you to discuss and analyse a particular topic, using evidence from the play to develop an argument in an organised, coherent and persuasive way. Examiners look for, and reward, what they call 'an informed personal response'. This simply means that you show you have good knowledge of the play ('informed') and can use evidence from it to support and justify your own viewpoint ('personal').

You can write about *Hamlet* from different points of view. As pages 85–105 show, you can approach the play from a number of critical perspectives (feminist, psychoanalytic, political, etc.). You can also set the play in its social, literary, political and other contexts. You should write at different levels, moving beyond description to analysis and evaluation. Simply telling the story or describing characters is not as effective as analysing how events or characters embody wider concerns of the play – its themes, issues, preoccupations, or, more simply, 'what the play is about'. In *Hamlet*, these wider concerns include revenge, delay, madness and corruption.

How should you answer an examination question or write a coursework essay? The following threefold structure can help you organise your response:

opening paragraph
developing paragraphs
concluding paragraph.

Opening paragraph. Begin with a paragraph identifying just what topic or issue you will focus on. Show that you have understood what the question is about. You probably will have prepared for particular topics. But look closely at the question and identify key words to see what particular aspect it asks you to write about. Adapt your material to answer that question. Examiners do not reward an essay, however well written, if it is not on the question set.

Developing paragraphs. This is the main body of your essay. In it, you develop your argument, point by point, paragraph by paragraph. Use evidence from the play that illuminates the topic or issue, and answers the question set. Each paragraph makes a point of dramatic or thematic significance. Some paragraphs could make points concerned with context or particular critical approaches. The effect of your argument builds up as each paragraph adds to the persuasive quality of your essay. Use brief quotations that support your argument, and show clearly just why they are relevant. Ensure that your essay demonstrates that you are aware that *Hamlet* is a play, a drama intended for performance and, therefore, open to a wide variety of interpretations and audience responses.

Concluding paragraph. Your final paragraph pulls together your main conclusions. It does not simply repeat what you have written earlier, but summarises concisely how your essay has successfully answered the question.

Example

Here is an example of how to put this structure into practice. In an examination it is usually helpful to prepare similar notes from which you write your essay, paragraph by paragraph. The following notes show the 'ingredients' of an answer. To help you understand how contextual matters or points from different critical approaches might be included, the words 'Context' or 'Criticism' appear before some items (but these would not appear in your essay). Remember that examiners are not impressed by 'name-dropping': use of critics' names. They want you to show your own knowledge and judgement of the play and its contexts, and your understanding of how it has been interpreted from different critical perspectives.

> Question: 'What importance do acting and actors have in the play as a whole?'

Opening paragraph

Show you are aware that the question asks for a discussion of both 'acting' and 'actors'. So include the following points and aim to write a sentence or more on each:

- The play is rich in language of acting and theatre: 'act', 'seem', 'show', 'play'.
- 'Acting' occurs throughout in many ways: characters pretend, spy and perform.
- 'Actors' are present both as the players and as all the characters who pretend and spy.
- The crucial importance of acting and actors can be understood by considering certain key examples (which you will look at in the paragraphs which follow).

Developing paragraphs

Now write a paragraph on each of a number of examples of 'acting and actors'. In each paragraph identify the importance (dramatic, thematic, etc.) of the example you are discussing. Some examples you might include are given briefly below. One aspect of the importance of each is given in brackets, but there are of course others.

- Hamlet begins by denying he is acting: 'I know not seems.' (But there is dramatic irony in his claim because he spends much of the play playing different roles.)
- Hamlet puts on 'an antic disposition'. (Other characters and the audience are unsure whether he is really mad or just pretending; this uncertainty increases the audience's interest.)
- Claudius keeps up the appearance of a capable and respected ruler. But what is behind the mask becomes more and more apparent. At prayer he reveals his guilt. He plans to have Hamlet executed in England; corrupts Laertes by involving him in the murderous plot of the duel, and lies to Gertrude about Laertes: 'How much I had to do to calm his rage!' (Dramatic tension heightens as his deceit and murderous nature are revealed.)

- Rosencrantz and Guildenstern put on an act of friendship. (Their unmasking can add to audience enjoyment, but their death raises worrying questions about the morality of Hamlet's apparent indifference to the fate of these two relatively innocent 'actors'.)
- Criticism: political Polonius acts as a concerned father and chief minister of state. (But he gives Reynaldo instructions to spy on his son, and he eavesdrops on Hamlet. His concern with surveillance results in his death. Surveillance is a pervasive theme.)
- Criticism: political Elsinore itself can be interpreted as 'acting'. (The ceremonial and festivities of Claudius' court conceals a rotten society.)
- Laertes pretends to act chivalrously in the duel, but intends murder. (His pretence is vital to plot development, leading to the death of Hamlet and Claudius.)
- Criticism: feminist Ophelia is forced to 'act' to enable her father and Claudius to eavesdrop on Hamlet: 'Read on this book'. But she, Gertrude and Horatio may be the only major characters who do not deliberately put on an act. (Their integrity contrasts with other characters' pretence, thus highlighting the importance of acting.)
- Criticism: performance The players embody the theme of pretence, and they are crucial to the plot. (The First Player's tears for Hecuba prompt Hamlet to devise his play-within-a-play, and its performance unmasks Claudius.)
- Context Hamlet's questioning of Rosencrantz and Guildenstern, and his advice to the players reveal significant aspects of acting and actors in Shakespeare's time.

Concluding paragraph

Write several sentences pulling together your conclusions. You might include the following points:

- Most characters put on an act of some kind: pretending, deceiving.
- Such pretence is a constant reminder of the theme of reality and appearance that runs through the play.
- Criticism: political Such deception contributes to the sense of corruption in Denmark.
- The players and the play-within-a-play are a crucial turning point in the plot. They make Claudius face up to his guilt, and convince Hamlet that the Ghost has spoken truthfully.

- **Context** Shakespeare's preoccupation with acting and actors is revealed, giving insight into aspects of theatre in Elizabethan London.
- **Criticism: performance** The play gives insight into Shakespeare's presentation of the multi-layered nature of performance and appearance. *Hamlet* can be interpreted as showing how Shakespeare uses acting and actors as metaphors throughout the play to achieve his dramatic purposes.

Writing about character

Much critical writing about *Hamlet* traditionally focused on characters as if they were living human beings. Today it is not sufficient just to describe their personalities. When you write about characters you will also be expected to show that they are dramatic constructs. That means that they embody the wider concerns of the play, have certain dramatic functions, and that they are set in a social and political world with particular values and beliefs.

All that may seem difficult and abstract. But don't feel overwhelmed. Everything you read in this book is written with those principles in mind, and can be a model for your own writing. Of course, you should say what a character seems like to you, but you should also set him or her in a context of some kind.

For example, you could describe Laertes as angry, or hot-headed and impulsive when he challenges Claudius and rebukes the Priest in the graveyard. But the concern he expresses to Claudius for the lack of ceremony in burying Polonius ('his obscure funeral') and his rebuke to the Priest at Ophelia's grave ('What ceremony else?') are Shakespeare's reminders of the older chivalric world of King Hamlet's day. In the same way, some of Laertes' actions and language are in the style of the traditional revenger of revenge tragedy ('To hell allegiance, vows to the blackest devil'). By making these connections, your writing places the characters in a social world, and identifies values or conventions that guide their behaviour. You are placing them 'in context'.

What a character says or does can be interpreted as reflecting some broader concern or some social, religious, moral or ethical code. Perhaps the clearest example is Hamlet's apparent inability to put the Ghost's command into practice: 'Revenge his foul and most unnatural murder'. He is inhibited by religious, social and moral objections to revenge. These constraints, and his doubts about the Ghost's nature, are further increased by Hamlet's scepticism, a way of thinking that in Shakespeare's time was challenging medieval ways of understanding and believing. Another 'context' point.

In *Hamlet*, as in all of Shakespeare's plays, individual and society are always interlinked. Hamlet and Fortinbras are sons who seek revenge, but are also princes caught up in political struggles. Personalities and personal relations have implications for matters of state. Shakespeare makes that interconnection clear in Rosencrantz' brief sentence:

> Never alone
> Did the king sigh, but with a general groan.
>
> *(Act 3 Scene 3, lines 22–3)*

Although Rosencrantz is flattering Claudius, his words clearly express that there is always a 'public' aspect of 'private' matters. The king's private anxieties ('sigh') have influence on, and are reflected in public matters. Society itself suffers ('a general groan') with the king. The implication for your writing is that you should, of course, discuss characters, but you should also try to show how they reflect and express much wider concerns and contexts.

Hamlet is subject to violent mood swings. He is dejected and pessimistic, elated, or calm and stoical. He also plays many roles, such as reflective philosopher, bloodthirsty revenger, self-critical actor, ironical observer, disgusted onlooker. But through the character of Hamlet Shakespeare explores social and political aspects of his time, and uses Hamlet to consider the nature of the individual self confronted with particular moral, ethical or religious predicaments.

Characters embody social, political and moral issues of significance to Shakespeare's society – and today's. Ophelia and Gertrude are fictional characters in a drama, but, as feminist criticism shows, they represent attitudes to gender in Elizabethan society. You should argue for your own view as to whether Polonius is shrewd or foolish, a loving or a harsh father (and show you are aware of interpretations different from your own). But your writing should also show that Polonius represents particular attitudes to political control, surveillance and patriarchy. Take Hamlet's advice and show how theatre reflects the form and pressure of the times!

As always, never forget that *Hamlet* is a play. Even though characters embody particular themes, Shakespeare's language gives actors many opportunities to play characters in all kinds of different ways. For example, Ophelia has been played as timid and obedient, an unprotesting victim of male power. But she has also been played as strong and resourceful, obeying her father, but clearly under protest.

A note on examiners

Examiners do not try to trap you or trick you. They set questions and select passages for comment intended to help you write your own informed personal response to the play. They expect your answer to display a sound knowledge and understanding of the play, and to be well structured. They want you to develop an argument, using evidence from the text to support your interpretations and judgements. Examiners know there is never one 'right answer' to a question, but always opportunities to explore different approaches and interpretations. They welcome answers which directly address the question set, but which show originality, insight and awareness of complexity. Above all, they reward responses that show your awareness that *Hamlet* is a play for performance, and that you can identify how Shakespeare achieves his dramatic effects.

And what about critics? Examiners want you to show you are aware of different critical approaches to the play. But they do not expect you simply to drop critics' names into your essay, or to remember quotations from critics. Rather, they want you to show that you can interpret the play from different critical perspectives, and that you know that any critical approach provides only a partial view of *Hamlet*. Often, that need only be just a part of your essay. In your writing, examiners are always interested centrally in your view of the play, and of how you have come to that view from thinking critically about the play, reading it, reading about it, seeing it performed, and perhaps from acting some of it yourself – even if that acting takes place in your imagination!

Resources

Books

A C Bradley, *Shakespearean Tragedy*, Penguin, 1991
Originally published in 1904, the most important source of 'character criticism'.

James L Calderwood, 'Verbal Presence: Conceptual Absence' in Martin Coyle (ed.), *New Casebooks: Hamlet*, Macmillan, 1992
A dense, typical example of postmodern (or deconstruction) criticism.

H B Charlton, *Shakespearean Tragedy*, Methuen, 1948
A clearly written introduction, mainly concerned with character, but calling for a synthesis of approaches to the tragedies.

Martin Coyle (ed.), *New Casebooks: Hamlet*, Macmillan, 1992
A valuable collection of modern criticism (contains the articles by Calderwood, Smith, Showalter and Tennenhouse noted in this book list).

Anthony B Dawson, *Shakespeare in Performance: Hamlet*, Manchester University Press, 1997
Discussion of over a dozen productions from three centuries, together with film versions; reveals great variation in interpretation and performance.

John Dover Wilson, *What Happens in Hamlet*, Cambridge University Press, 1935
This discussion of Elizabethan attitudes to *Hamlet* is still helpful and relevant.

Terry Eagleton, *William Shakespeare*, Basil Blackwell, 1986
Although Eagleton includes only a few pages on *Hamlet*, his book exemplifies postmodern (or deconstructive) approaches to Shakespeare's plays.

Harley Granville-Barker, *Prefaces to Shakespeare. Hamlet*, Batsford, 1963
A highly influential reading of the play by a theatre practitioner.

Andrew Gurr and Mariko Ichikawa, *Staging in Shakespeare's Theatres*, Oxford University Press, 2000
An authoritative account of the major features of Elizabethan playhouses. A long chapter conjectures how *Hamlet* was first staged at the Globe in 1601.

Robert Hapgood (ed.), *Shakespeare in Production: Hamlet*, Cambridge University Press, 1999
Tells the story of *Hamlet* in production from Burbage at the Globe to Kenneth Branagh's film. Links stage interpretations to developments in theatre, criticism and society.

Michael Hattaway, *Hamlet: The Critics Debate*, Macmillan, 1987
A stimulating critical review of modern approaches, sharply aware of the social shaping of criticism and stage interpretations.

Russell Jackson (ed.), *The Cambridge Companion to Shakespeare on Film*, Cambridge University Press, 2000
At least five chapters contain helpful discussions of films of *Hamlet*.

John Jump (ed.), *Shakespeare: Hamlet, a Casebook*, Macmillan, 1968
A valuable selection of traditional criticism from 1710–1964.

Frank Kermode, *Shakespeare's Language*, Allen Lane, Penguin, 2000
A detailed examination of how Shakespeare's language changed over the course of his playwriting career. The chapters on the major tragedies are full of helpful detail.

Victor Kiernan, *Eight Tragedies of Shakespeare: A Marxist Study*, Verso, 1996
Argues that Shakespeare's personal experience is expressed in his plays as sympathy for the poor.

L C Knights, *An Approach to Hamlet*, Chatto and Windus, 1960
A harsh judgement of Hamlet's character, rooted in close attention to language.

Jan Kott, *Shakespeare Our Contemporary*, Methuen, 1965
An influential political reading of Shakespeare's plays. Much criticised today, but performance and criticism still take account of Kott's ground-breaking study.

Michael Pennington, *Hamlet: A User's Guide*, Nick Hern, 1996
A practical introduction by an actor who has appeared in over 600 performances of the play. Very readable, with many theatrical insights.

Elaine Showalter, 'Representing Ophelia: Women, Madness and the Responsibilities of Feminist Criticism', in Martin Coyle (ed.), *New Casebooks: Hamlet*, Macmillan, 1992
Shows how portrayals of Ophelia have embodied male attitudes to female sexuality and madness.

Rebecca Smith, 'A Heart Cleft in Twain: the Dilemma of Shakespeare's Gertrude', in Martin Coyle (ed.), *New Casebooks: Hamlet*, Macmillan, 1992
A feminist reading which challenges conventional portrayals of Gertrude as vain, self-satisfied and lustful.

Caroline Spurgeon, *Shakespeare's Imagery and What it Tells Us*, Cambridge University Press, 1935
Spurgeon's identification of image-clusters as a dominant feature of the plays has influenced later studies.

Leonard Tennenhouse, 'Power in *Hamlet*', in Martin Coyle (ed.), *New Casebooks: Hamlet*, Macmillan, 1992

A demanding essay on the political implications of the rival claims to power of Hamlet and Claudius.

G Wilson Knight, *The Wheel of Fire*, Methuen, 1949

Contains two essays on *Hamlet*: 'Hamlet's Melancholia' and 'The Embassy of Death', which argues that Claudius is essentially a good man and Hamlet 'an element of evil in the state of Denmark'.

Films

Over 50 films of *Hamlet* or adaptations of the play have been made. The films listed below are usually available on video or DVD (but distributors sometimes restrict availability in certain countries). Only the 1996 Kenneth Branagh film offers a full text. All others cut the text significantly, and often rearrange episodes.

Hamlet (UK, 1948) Director: Laurence Olivier. Laurence Olivier (Hamlet).

Hamlet (USSR, 1964) Director: Grigori Kozintszev. Innokenti Smoktunovski (Hamlet).

Hamlet (USA, 1964) Directors: Bill Colleran, John Gielgud. Richard Burton (Hamlet).

Hamlet (UK, 1969) Director: Tony Richardson. Nicol Williamson (Hamlet).

Hamlet (UK, 1990) Director: Franco Zeffirelli. Mel Gibson (Hamlet).

Hamlet (UK, 1996) Director: Kenneth Branagh. Kenneth Branagh (Hamlet).

Hamlet (USA, 2000) Director: Michael Almereyda. Ethan Hawke (Hamlet).

Audio books

Three major versions are easily available, in the series produced by:

Naxos (Hamlet: Anton Lesser)

Arkangel (Hamlet: Simon Russell Beale)

HarperCollins (Hamlet: Paul Scofield)

Hamlet on the Web

If you type 'Hamlet Shakespeare' into your search engine, it will find over 100,000 items. Because websites are of wildly varying quality, and rapidly disappear or are created, no recommendation can safely be made here. But if you have time to browse, you may find much of interest.